Contents

The Riddles
of
Aleister Crowley

Amado Crowley

Published by Diamond Books, 29 High Street, Great Bookham, Leatherhead, Surrey.

First edition 1992

ISBN 0-9517528-1-2

Printed in Great Britain by BPCC Wheatons Ltd, Exeter

PREFACE

In May, 1991, I published the first book on the life and work of my father, and I called it 'The Secrets of Aleister Crowley'. The book I present now is not so much a sequel as an addendum. I have more things to say, other affairs to divulge, and new insights to give into his secret truths.

As far as possible, I have kept this second book independent of the first. What I mean is: you don't need to have read the one in order to understand the other. That is my hope anyway. But as the Scottish poet, Robert Burns put it: "the best laid schemes o' mice an' men gang aft a-gley." Some readers may be puzzled. To help them, I begin this preface with an overview of the major points in that first book.

1. Some seventeen years before his death, Aleister Crowley made plans for my birth. He chose my mother with care and arranged for me to be conceived near Boulogne, France. My mother married a young admirer but they were not happy. A few years later, she got a legal separation on the grounds of cruelty.

2. Aleister Crowley gave me a 'magical education' from the age of seven to fourteen. After I was made an Initiate, he sent me back into hiding. His orders were to stay concealed until I received 'the call'.

3. I was taught things that do not exist in his books. He said that he only ever published anything when he was short of money! As if to stress the point, he made it clear that he did not expect me to read them. I would find no pearls of wisdom, he said. There was no harm in them, but not much help either. This made it clear that there was a great gap between his public and private teaching.

4. Gerald Gardener paid my father by the page to design the bible of the witches: 'The Book of Shadows'. After my father's death, in 1947, Gardner issued a false account of his own. Since the western world is now thick with witch groups, this news must be irksome. But Crowley built 'a gateway' into the system, through which genuine seekers could find a path.

5. 'The Book of the Law' was a hoax, meant to conceal a more important discovery: 'The Book of Desolation'. He kept the second book secret and never once hinted of its existence. Other antique writings point to this one and some scholars have had a whiff of its existence. The book is in my care. I have not yet met the next Guardian. The critics of Crowley admit he was sincere in his beliefs. Thus it is clear that his faking of 'The

Book of the Law' was done for good reason. Since one great discovery was on open sale, nobody would think of looking for the other one.

6. In the Second World War, Crowley was used in an operation to coax Rudolf Hess to abandon Hitler. This was apart of a more ornate plan to revive the Hapsburg Empire and put Lord Louis Mountbatten on the throne. This would have provided a bulwark against any communist plans for taking over South East Europe.

7. Far from being a bitter enemy of the Russian mystic, Gurdjieff, he was a friendly rival. Not only do their notions overlap, but they contain much of the same material. When Gurdjieff 'vanished' from Paris just before the Germans marched in, Aleister Crowley found him shelter at Frinton, on the Essex coast in England.

Of course, Aleister Crowley knew that he would be betrayed or abandoned by his 'friends', so he needed a scion to succeed him - someone to whom he could entrust his work. He gave me a stack of papers and the book mentioned earlier. I was told to reveal them only to persons who asked a certain question. In fifty years of waiting, nobody has done so.

I have met many 'students of the occult' who have put me through their little tests. None of them realized that I was testing them. This is why I scorn my father's enemies, and mock their slurs on his private life. They have done all they could to wipe out his memory and his words. But he remains the greatest single Magus of his time.

Given his reasons for writing them, my father's books are difficult to understand. One has to know the code, and one works very hard to make very little headway. Like Van Gogh's candle, or Dali's draped watches, there is a subtle symbolism. When Raphaël painted hands making odd gestures, he may not have been totally conscious of the reason. But when Crowley uses terms like law, will, love, daemon etc, he is painting a verbal rebus. There's lots of padding, of course. There's plenty of surplus material that has been just chucked in to set the tone. His style is tortured and heavy, except in his poetry and novels.

His occult texts were written mainly for money. But his poems and novels were written from his heart. Critics look only at the erotic surface and do not see the veiled meaning. It amused him, having that type of mind, to slip in all manner of mystic codes, clues and puzzles. It made him smile to think of all the occult snobs who would miss the point. They sit in libraries and pore over the texts, muttering his words as if they are mantras or a sacred breviary. And they are blinded by their own opinions.

That is not the way to go about it. Yes, there are enigmas, acronyms and acrostics galore but those are mainly his own sense of fun. The gold is spread so thinly as to go almost unseen. If you dig too brutally, you miss it - and if you miss it, you end up by imposing your own meanings on my father's words. This is why people get it wrong. This is why they have missed the main thread. Do you really think that a man of his stature spent his whole life speaking of mysteries which any yob could grasp from a paperback? If anyone asks for my advice, I just say this: "Watch your step. *He left* the Golden Dawn, remember!"

I dare say none of this sounds very reverent. But that's the whole point about Crowley: he was just about the most tactless man I ever knew. It is hard to be po-faced about it. It is stupid to behave like a funeral director giving the price of coffins. I know what Crowley was up to. But, as during the era when alcohol was banned in America, the gangsters moved in and created the occult speak-easy where they peddled their magic hooch. There are scores of pseudo experts, phoney groups and false orders. All of them are contrary to the law which Crowley set forth.

Aleister taught me the path that he believed in. No one else was quite so lucky. He himself put it this way: "You are the only student to have ridden the dragon, without being taken to the circus." The penny didn't drop until several years after his death, when I read his books just out of a sense of loyalty. Then it struck me, as clearly as if he had poked his finger into my eye. He had given me the secret of flight, while everyone else just walked. I had a ticket to soar through the clouds, whereas they just hobbled under a painted sunset. Their path and mine were not even aligned. They lead to different goals which are very wide apart.

Well, that's all it takes to make the old gang resent me. Their ranks have thinned. There are not too many left. At the same time, they are concerned. They imagine that I am putting new wine into old bottles and yet they have never tasted it. It is sublime wine. I was raised in the same vineyard, ripened under the same sun! I am not made as an investment to be kept in a cellar. This wine is for drinking, and I come from a good vintage. You, with your boring, tedious rituals and your embalmed beliefs: have you been reborn yet? But imagine what we would achieve by working together: we could give the Sphinx her voice again and set her singing so that the sands would bloom. We could hold back the mighty river and set it flowing along its ancient course once more.

If my words seem strange, that does not mean they are wrong.

Do you like your prophets to be dressed in rags, to have blazing eyes, and to have crackling skies above their heads? Are you looking for something a bit more 'Hollywood'? Think well before you reject me. When argument is done, I am the son of Master Therion. When you have finished your erudite chunter, I have risen from his ashes. Should you not rejoice? Are you truly meant to flee? Write me no more tomes on whether magic works or not. Give me no more shallow articles on whether occultism truly exists. I am here. I wait. I smile at the human tragedy and weep at the farce.

You are the ones who must write the future. Shall I act as your clerk, or shall you learn the A B C?

I am in my sixties now. I potter about the wrinkled, old world and shake my head at the futility of the creams and cosmetics. You want to look your best when the end comes. When the last trump sounds, you'll need to take a quick glance in the mirror. Pat you hair, this is God. Fix your tie or your hem-line, this is the Devil. Ask them what their job is. They'll ask you what you did for a living.

Many years ago, one of my own students said: "Beware of a Wizard's wrath!" I told him not to be so silly because I like people to relax and behave naturally. But I find he was right after all. Shortly after my first book was published, some people in or near Plymouth, in England, stole the cover design to 'plug' a commercial event. They cheated me. They defiled my father's image. They put my book in a bad light and I was angry. There is no point taking legal action; why go to all that expense when I have got means of my own? I wasn't going to ask the Gods to intervene either; why should they when they have bigger matters to deal with. I have a much better idea. Why don't I rely on truly neutral judges? Better still, why not make use of judges who are slightly biased in favour of the accused? That way, no one could ever accuse me of being unfair.

That is why I directed my call to the most open minds of all. I invoked and I summoned their own dead.

The words that follow are printed in reverse to stop your eye from reading them out of pure habit. These words will not loose their magic power by chance. If you have not hurt me, then these words will not hurt you. But if you have injured me, then by all means - have a good read. May your eyes be drawn. May your head be unable to turn away. This piece of magic hails from the North of England where I was born and spent all of my childhood. Those who know about such things call it Thorn Canker.

iv

,wac ... tebbig a no nevar a ekiL
,wam ... daeh sseleye na ta gnipwaG
,pans ... niks nwo sti kcep lliw luos yhT
!palf ... der snur tliug neddih lliT

If you think this is a joke, that's fine by me. If you prefer your world to be warm, cosy and reasonable, that's fine too. But if you expect all occult Masters to behave like plaster saints, you'll be aghast that I want vengeance. But there are laws, my friends. These laws are meant to defend us from evil and to keep us from doing evil. It is my duty to tell you that Life does not resemble 'Mary Poppins', with flowers and pink rabbits everywhere. What would be the point? What would be the meaning? Come, come! In the real world, April does not last for ever.

You remember Alice ... the girl in Lewis Carroll's book, 'Alice Through the Looking Glass'? She it was who stepped through the limits of reality and entered the other world which became "curiouser and curiouser", if you recall. I began writing this book in July, 1991. In November, 1991, the British police made raids in and around the city of Plymouth. I heard on the BBC news that some thirty-six people were arrested for dealing in drugs. Do you still say I am too severe?

Ah well! This book might be more interesting than the last one! But as Lewis Carroll would say: this is the last one. But not for very long! I shall soon be starting on another.

1

SIA

The god of the seeing mind

Armchair Critics
Some of the things I describe in my books may seem very exciting, especially if yours has been a peaceful, ordinary life. Indeed, you might be tempted to think that the whole story is far too strange to be true. Certainly, some individuals have found it so and have taken the trouble to drop me a line. Oh yes, that is one of the hazards of writing a book ... one gets letters ... lots of letters. To be quite fair, none of them have been nasty or offensive. On the contrary, they bend over backwards to be polite. That might just be part of keeping a wary space between them and the magician to whom they are talking. Even so, their meaning is quite clear. What they are actually saying is: "*Are you sure you've got it right?*" or "*Come, come, dear chap, aren't you letting your fancy run away with you?*"

I have heard from men who knew my father, who were in the Secret Services at the time, and who confirm all the statements that I have made. I am also sought by TV companies who want to make films out of my book. Other authors get in touch with me too, they wonder if I can help their research in some parallel topic. All in all, I am quite pleased with the reception my book has had.

But one gentleman was clearly upset.

"There seems on first reading to be a glaring anomaly which must raise questions. I refer to the statement supposedly made by Aleister on page 55: "*God bless America and wipe out the Vietcong*" - a highly prophetic statement since Aleister died in 1947?"

I recognized the subdued irony and wrote to him at once. I told him that I already knew when my father died, and confirmed that he had indeed made the odd prophecy now and again. So as not to cause offence, I did not mention that "anomaly" is a term used in astronomy for any weird motion of a celestial body. If the gentleman had been comparing me to a star, I ought to have been very flattered. But I'm fairly sure that this was not his intention. By a pure slip of the memory, he had chosen the wrong word. What he meant to point out was that there was a very clear *anachronism*. In using the word 'Vietcong', it looked as if my father was talking about an event twenty years in the future. The reader found this a bit too much to swallow!

Now the book was edited several times and at various stages during the project. One can miss spelling errors, printing errors and misuse of commas. But questions of fact are very rarely wrong. For example, I made several checks of the exact date on which the name of the Royal House of England was changed. Even in this book, I had to correct the date of Queen Victoria's death ... I had got it wrong, you see. You may be quite sure that if that use of the word 'Vietcong' had been an error, it would have been noticed.

As I readily admit, one failed to catch every small error, and could weep with fury. But all facts had been looked at and thought about. Now it must be obvious that if an error of this magnitude had indeed slipped past my eyes unnoticed, then I would have admitted it. If I were too proud for that, I might have tried to explain it away, e.g., I had used my own terms to clothe Aleister's sense, or else I had focussed on his emotions rather than his exact words. But no. I told the truth. And the truth is often much more difficult to accept.

Aleister did make prophetic remarks. He made them throughout his life. There are several other examples in my first book, and I offer even more of them in this volume. I have done this with full awareness. I meant to show one more aspect of my father's weird abilities. My error (if indeed it was an error) lay in not making these points much more obvious. I should have stressed them, or had them printed in red. The gentleman in question had noticed only one of them and made the wrong guess. I had expected some trouble about my claim that Aleister and I walked into the air from the path along the Dover cliffs. But no comment at all. Not a sausage about Crowley's use of magic.

It is one of the hazards of being an author that readers have the eyes of a hawk and will pounce on the smallest slip. They do not write books themselves, or else they would not bother. But it seems to give them great pleasure to drop a kindly note to let an author know that he has dropped a brick. I have to confess that I did it myself with Colin Wilson once. I was much younger then. I even liked him then. But it turned out not to have been an author's error but one caused by the printers. I felt very small and I never wrote to him or any other author again.

But it does pay to be very careful. One must not be slip-shod or skimp one's work. There is a whole tribe of these amateur critics and very few of them ever think to enclose the return postage. I suppose they think that having gone to the expense of writing to you, it is only fair that you should do the same. Well, they are quite wrong. No one is obliged to answer letters which have not been invited. If I do it, then I do it out of pure courtesy. But even then I only do it once. Good manners can leave one penniless.

The Gallant Naval Officer

But there is no avoiding the fact that half a century has gone by, and perhaps one's memory "touches up" some bits and plays down others. But then again, no matter how it may seem to you, Aleister Crowley did live an exciting life. He upset the climate of his times, just as Hurricane Charlie might rip across the isobars of the weather map on television. He was a man who upset and daunted people, so it's small wonder that his life story should read like Baron Munchausen or James Bond. As a matter of fact, the man who wrote the James Bond novels was on very good terms with my father. I am referring, of course, to the late Ian Fleming himself.

It is common knowledge that Fleming was a member of Naval Intelligence. Through his contacts with Maxwell Knight, he tried to persuade Churchill to let Crowley talk to Hess after he had landed in Scotland. Fleming was convinced that Hess would open up to him and not to anyone else. Hess was a student of magic and held Crowley in very high respect, not least because of his standing as regards the O.T.O.[1]

But the British government had had more than enough of Crowley. All the time he'd been working for them, they had been

1. Ordo Templi Orientis.

3

holding their breath so the sooner they broke the connection, the easier they would feel. In addition to which, Crowley had got to know about the other part of the scheme. This was worked out by Churchill and Roosevelt to put Lord Louis Mountbatten on the throne of the Hapsburg Empire.

But Maxwell Knight, the Head of the British Secret Services, had quite an interest in occultism and was very taken by Crowley. When the official link was cut on the orders of the War Cabinet, the personal link was maintained. They stayed good friends quite unbeknown to anyone else. It is my personal belief that Knight asked for Crowley's advice on other war-time operations. In this respect, it does not do to forget that Crowley was something of an expert on France and on the organization of the resistance networks.

Ian Fleming was actually in on both the official plot and the private schemes. He quite liked both men, and neither of them objected to Fleming's love of the fast life and high jinks. As a matter of fact, Fleming felt ashamed of the way that Aleister had been treated by Churchill and also by Mountbatten. "Shabby!" I heard him declare. "Downright, bloody shabby!" In his own small way, he was trying to make it up to my father.

Certainly, Aleister quite approved of him, considering him to be "a gentleman, with great personal honour". I think he also liked Fleming's unalloyed joy in sex, food and thrills. "You could well have been an occultist," Aleister once told him. Fleming gave them all a shock when he answered: "I consider that I am."

A Student of Crowley?

I didn't find Fleming to be in any way a debauched man. My father said he was very strict, even ruthless with himself and "quite able to stick to the regime I gave him." These words didn't quite register at the time, but turning it over later, it suggests that Fleming was 'in training' for something, and that Aleister Crowley was his 'coach'. Now I grant that my father had once been a first class mountain climber, but that was much earlier in life. The only subjects on which he was an expert were (a) occultism and (b) magic. Make of that what you will.

In my own opinion, and I am not a scholar of literature, Ian Fleming spells out some of his own, personal values through his most famous character: James Bond, 007. Yes, I know that the books were works of fiction. I am also aware that the character is supposed to have been based on a certain fellow he knew. Even so, I think there is a great deal of Ian Fleming in him - even to the slight hint of ambiguity in 007's approach to sex.

No, I am not saying that Ian Fleming was bi-sexual, whatever that might mean. I am not even hinting at it. In his own way, I think he rose above that kind of facile label. Let us simply say that he didn't find men, as such, the least bit repugnant. I leave the matter there. In any case, I regard James Bond as an image of Ian Fleming's 'hidden' side. The exploits are unreal. The habits and aspect of the character are based on someone else. Even so, the author's own persona is quite evident.

Aleister told me that Ian Fleming's motto could well have been "*Why Not?*", and that this was not terribly far from the spirit of the Law of Thelema. This may be why the women in his Bond novels are often highly athletic, almost as skilled and as deadly as young men. And don't you find that in some of the romantic situations, James Bond seems to indulge or savour a slight taste for the rough approach? Is he an expert in S & M?[2]

To the best of my knowledge, it was Dennis Wheatley who first drew Crowley to the attention of Admiral Godfrey. But Wheatley was also a good friend of Fleming. No doubt it took combined, muscular effort to persuade the top-brass that a person of such repute as Crowley could be of value in their unfolding plans. I can't remember where I got the knowledge, but I have always thought that it was Ian Fleming who went to and fro between London and Lisbon. He acted as our go between with the two Germans[3] who helped to set up the Hess project. Fleming would have cut no ice with them unless they knew that he spoke for my father.

But Ian Fleming was not used in any of the dealings with the Papal Emissary. Someone felt that he might overstep the limits of protocol, with his pert words and his casual, play-boy attitude. Which makes it all the more intriguing then that they let my father come face to face with the Dean of Vatican Diplomats! But the person in question knew all about Crowley and, being an occultist himself[4], he himself may have insisted on the meeting.

As is obvious from Ian Fleming's books, he hated Hitler as

2. Sado-masochism.
3. Karl Haushoffer and Joseph Retinger.
4. This was the then Bishop Roncalli, who later became Pope John XXIII.

much as other men hated the Devil. He was so adamant in his wish to destroy Hitler, that his seniors wondered if he might not overstep the limit and act too rashly. A man who is writing Ian Fleming's biography told me that Fleming paid out of his own pocket for an astrologer to send lies from Berne to Hess.[5] The man was this keen for the allied plans to work.

Fleming had some trouble getting the tame astrologer to agree a just fee. My father said: "Tell him I have followers in Zurich and I shall send them to throttle him!" For all I know, Fleming might have done just that.

Bluebells and The Phallus of Thoth
At all events, Ian Fleming was present in person at the 'firework display'. This was Aleister's way of referring to the magic ceremony which took place in Ashdown Forest to entice Hess. He was so impressed by this that, even though sworn to secrecy, he made reference to it in his books (and the films). Certainly, Ian Fleming had total faith in the success of the elaborate plan. He hadn't the slightest doubt that Rudolf Hess would come in answer to this ardent call. Indeed, I believe it was Fleming who persuaded the Duke of Hamilton to allow his name to be used as part of the bait.[6] As a result, he was extremely excited, almost drunk on pure adrenalin.

There is much to suggest that Fleming was himself an occultist. But as to whether he was a follower of Aleister Crowley or not ... I can only surmise. I suspect that this was the case. But I've nothing very solid to go on. He addressed my father as "Master" and me as "Amado". Even if people hesitated to tease my father, they would quite happily play jokes with me. I was only a child, and I wasn't likely to take offence. In spite of that, Fleming was always - how can I put it? - he was very 'correct', ... in the same way that a court Equerry might be when waiting on a child prince.

He did one very charming thing which lends a little support to my opinions in this direction. When AC was so harshly dropped after the Hess affair, Fleming sent him a gift of a bottle of toilet water from Trumps, or Trumpers, in Mayfair. It has always

---

5. Louis de Wohl, the Hungarian astrologer, was employed mainly to provide The War Cabinet with the kind of advice that Hitler would be getting from his personal astrologer.
6. see: Chapter 16.

6

stayed in my mind because of the simple fact that it was called 'Bluebell Tonic' or 'Bluebell Lotion'. I can't quite get all the words, but certainly it had something to do with bluebells. He enclosed a small note on which was written the simple reference: 'King John IV.ii.11'.

This is not one of Shakespeare's most popular plays. But if one looks up this particular passage, this is what one finds:-

To gild refined gold, to paint the lily,
To throw a perfume on the violet,
To smooth the ice, or add another hue
Unto the rainbow, or with a taper light
To seek the beauteous eye of heaven to garnish,
Is wasteful and ridiculous excess.

Ian Fleming was keen enough on magic to have had deep talks with my father, often in the company of Dennis Wheatley. Wheatley had known my father much longer than the others, and had pumped him for material on black magic for use in his famous novels[7]. You will surely recognize my father's unique touch when the baddies in the book are hunting for the shrunken 'Phallus of Thoth', and the goodies are trying to stop them. Honestly! *The Phallus of Thoth!* How on earth did he get away with that one?[8]

7. e.g. The Devil Rides Out, 1936.
8. As a matter of academic interest, this name "Thoth" should be pronounced as if written "Tay-hoo-tea".

7

2

PE AND NEKHEN

The watchful ancestors of a living prince

Understanding

I sent a nice little article to a Swiss magazine some three or four years ago. As is quite common with that special magazine, they did not reply and we were obliged to telephone them. I think it was their way of cutting down on expenses. They did not discuss the merits or demerits of the article itself. That wasn't what worried them. They were terribly concerned that I had signed myself "Master".

"Masters are secretive," they said.

"What makes you think that?" I asked.

"Masters do not designate themselves," they replied.

"Nor have I," I said. "I was chosen."

"If you were chosen, we would have known about it."

"How so, if Masters are secretive?" I asked.

They never did publish my article. It makes one wonder why on earth Albert Einstein ever chose to work in that country. The more I think about it, the better I understand why the Vatican has its Swiss Guard - all equipped with chest x-rays, of course.[1] My father did visit Switzerland from time to time - "for the sake of my health", as he put it. "You just cross the frontier, and you feel so much happier when you come back."

Of course, there are some Swiss occultists who really and truly believe that AC accepted their bona fides and that he told them all that they wanted to know. They did not know their Crowley though. "To be praised by the Swiss is rather like having your physique admired by a cannibal," he said. "It makes one wonder

1. To obtain permission to work in Switzerland, even for two weeks, you have to undergo a medical and they x-ray every part of you either to guard against disease or to see if you are hiding any gold on your person. Also, if you try to make them laugh you have got to say: "Das is der englische joke!"

if America, after all, is not a better place to be. But then, neither one nor the other could ever be called subtle."

To get the best out of Crowley, (or out of me, for that matter) it was very much a question of adopting the proper approach. I am told by karate experts that one should not face one's opponent like someone about to do the ski-jump. Similarly in the theatre, as in life, the lad who plays Romeo should not confront Juliet as if he were the world's best chicken plucker! Well, it is very much the same with an occult Master. There is no need to approach him in a crawling position, with tongue out, ready to lick his boots. But neither should you pretend that the premises belong to you and start tossing him scraps.

If I may offer you some counsel: do not patronise him. But do not try to lord it over him either. Scrap yards, knacker's yards and graveyards all do exist, I'm afraid. But for over-bold students we have made a special deal with a zoo on the astral plane. Your best bet is to show respect in the way you behave, stand and speak. Only a numskull would go out of his way to be rude.

Dealing with Masters

Occult masters are not all that common. Well, there are fewer of them than, say, outlets for American fast-food chains. Somehow or other the term 'outlet' seems just the right word. On the other hand, they are not as rare as honest men of politics or courteous civil servants. Let's put it this way: there are always enough to meet the need. Today, the need isn't all that great! Most people make do with pop-singers and the embalmed stars of television soap operas. They look for the spot-light and not a halo.

Aleister Crowley had some quite strong views on teaching others or acting as their guide:

"I have no time to argue. It is as simple as that. We cannot afford any discussion at all. If you think about it, you will see that this is the trouble with the Socratic method! I don't know why, but students seem to forget that we are all dying a little more each day."

This was not a morbid man, I must add. This was someone who was being a realist when all those who approached him were looking for a dreamer. This was a man who was only too vividly aware of the value of time, the cost of each day, and the errors in all known theories of education.

9

"In its infinite wisdom, "That World There and Then" has made some people 'Seekers of Truth' and others 'Speakers of Truth'. There is no need to cut tokens from cornflake packets and send for a prize. You sit. I talk. You learn. I teach. I have not striven all my life just to listen to you airing your views. Nor does it help to further the Great Work, to give students the pleasure of showing where truth is wrong. You must sit at my knees and be thankful I don't send you packing!"

On a good day he would explain a little further.

"If you do not like my attitudes or my methods, that is quite all right - as long as you stay silent. If you do not allow yourself to understand what I say, then we shall play chess instead. That way you will learn nothing of any great value but you will at least help me pass the time amiably. If you don't play chess, I advise you to get sawn in half!"

"Your social standing does not really matter, any more than your level of formal schooling. What counts with a Master is your soul. 'Are you open?' is the first question he asks. 'Are you innocent?' is the second. He does not have any opinions and he will find it painful if you insist on sharing your own. 'It is less arduous to teach a person who knows nothing,' he will say, 'than a self-taught individual who thinks that he knows everything.' For that one reason alone, he prefers young folk. They are rash, fearful, naive and proud - but they will swap their deepest beliefs the moment they find something 'better'."

I was young, remember: seven years old when I met him, and fourteen when we said goodbye. But he has stayed with me all my life. It was more than talk, of course. He did magic. It was like catching hold of a high-speed train and being whisked out of one reality, into another, yet always able to understand both. An apprenticeship in magic may sound as if he washed my brain! You should be so lucky! It is not passive. There is no mad surgeon popping new bits and pieces into your numbed nervous system at random. You work. You strive. You try to renounce your old persona like a serpent sloughing its skin, and you pray to emerge not just changed but made unsoiled.

It is easier to have second thoughts than to let yourself begin. It is easier to withdraw than to dread that you might fail. It is easier to kill yourself than to be reborn to life. It is easier by far to jump through the eye of a needle.[2]

Friends and Cheats

I was meant to be Crowley's 'little secret'. As things have turned out, I am far from 'little' and, it is a long time now since I discovered it was impossible to stay 'secret'. It wasn't easy keeping my mouth shut as a child. It seemed more important then to be proud, and to have something to brag about. Crowley let a few of his closest friends 'in' on the matter and, to be quite fair, they never told a soul.

But this is why, when Crowley died, he did not mention me in any will. He left me nothing, or perhaps I'd better say: he left me nothing of any material value. If any of his dubious friends got wind of my existence, it was easy for them to dismiss me as just one more bastard.

But as Edmund says[3]: "I grow, I prosper; Now, Gods, stand up for bastards!" When the old man had died, they divided up the spoils. This one got one thing, that one got another, and I got a walking stick, insight into his secret teachings, the things I listed earlier - and authority.

So far as I know, none of those old cronies lost anything by going to his funeral. But neither I, nor any of the other children, gained so much as a penny - and some of us could well have done with it. Or let me put it another way: the death of Crowley enabled a few of the survivors to set themselves up as experts. He has changed their lives; of course, because, like gurus on any other subject (Shakespeare for example, Chaucer or the Bible), they have lived under the shadow of their topic. I should think they have been well pleased with the financial return on their labours. But at the spiritual level though - how can I put it? - *"whence comes the flame when the candle has been snuffed out?"*

I call them old cronies. That is because they are now old men, if indeed they are still alive. When they knew Crowley, they were younger. Were they also more loyal? Like most young men, I dare say, they were utterly sincere and meant every word they said. With age, one is less rash and more foolish, and the wind changes direction less often. The times grow cold and the sunny sparkle dims. Just as children outgrow their dreams and their

---

2. cf. Matthew 19:21.
3. Shakespeare, King Lear, I. ii.

11

heroes, so grown men can forget their zeal and fervour. A former friend is now someone you once knew. A love that all but crucified your soul becomes a girl you once went out with. It is never a sudden act of treason; it is a slow casual crossing of no-man's land.

It was after he had died that they began to renegue. Or let me put it this way: very few of them spoke well of their departed friend and Master. Hardly any of them had anything nice to say. I find that rather odd. Did they simply changed their minds? Or did they perhaps change sides too? How else can one explain it? As far as I can tell, Aleister has not done them the least harm. He didn't come back either to haunt them, or to scrounge one more loan of money. Are we to presume then that there always was a slight grudge? And were they in the habit of keeping it well and truly hidden? Has it really taken all of fifty years to rise to the surface?

As you know, there are spots, boils, carbuncles and furuncles that all do much the same thing. A sub-virus sleeps in your skin from infancy and then, suddenly, it erupts in flaming red and very painful lesions all over your body without reason. Maybe it is the same with ancient spite. Maybe the boils are a form of 'just desserts' brought about by past deceits. They hit the prophet Job, didn't they? They even blasted the skin of Pharaoh and the Egyptians! Who knows? They might even strike in that earthly paradise called Zurich.

On my father's behalf, and in my father's seat, I call them to account. "Their reasons for doing what they did are not to their credit and the ravenous Hawk shrieks in the mountains."

We can stop bluffing when someone dies, we can stop paying lip service to all the old lies. Even lice will tell you, there is nothing to be gained by hanging on! But it is one thing to abandon a fallen leader, and quite another to join the enemy. The ones who devised the lies would ruin his life's work.

Upstairs, Downstairs[4]
If I had done Crowley such wrong, I would not sleep easy at night. He made his plans. If the revenge seems long in coming, that's because he is making it perfect. If it were me, I'd put matters straight before I detected that wheeze of asthma or sniffed

---

4. A distinction once made between family and servants.

the cologne from that little shop in Mayfair. If one tries to justify the deed, one is not saying sorry. But they will discover how much easier it is to express regret when standing on the scaffold.

"You are old, Father William, the young man cried,
And pleasures with youth pass away,
And yet you lament not the days that are gone,
Now tell me the reason, I pray."[5]

The attacks on Crowley have grown into a real campaign that has gone on for years and years. Even those former friends might have begun to wonder. But that is the point about agit-prop, is it not, to try and change opinion? Those who stayed with him right from the start, very rarely renegued. Rather it was the newcomers, those whose contact had been brief, who had second thoughts. There is a certain one of these who, like Hamlet's mother, protests too much as he stashes the loot behind halo and wings. Though he cakes himself with incense or rolls up one leg of his trousers, he hasn't the authority to pardon himself, and he will never feel heart's-ease. He let the cock crow a hundred times. He played Judas without being asked! Like a rose-red tart or the whore of Babylon, he kissed and gladly told!

There was no such burden on me. I was not faced with any such decision. Nobody tempted me to reprint the books of Aleister Crowley - which as I say have scant occult value, since they were inspired by an empty wallet. My mother and I were very poor. It didn't seem difficult at the time, but looking back I sometimes feel the clutch of fear. How often we were hungry. How dreary it was when we only had some chestnuts from my grandad on the table. We were in no position to exploit my father's name. We had a greater moral right than many others who lived in relative luxury. But we held on. God knows how, but my mother managed to hold on.

In the woollen mill where she worked, she sold sweets and peanuts, and with the small profit she bought me extra food. The pinnacle of the week was to meet my grandma on Friday outside the mill where she worked. We'd eat together at a café in the Market Hall. Our treat was called 'pie and gravy'. There was a comic drawing of a pig that gave the impression it was pork. We didn't know what it was really, and nobody asked. We weren't even sure it was meat. But I loved it. I adored it. I licked the

5. Robert Southey (1774-1843): 'The Old Man's Comforts, and how he gained them.'

13

gravy from the plate and nobody had the heart to correct my manners.

When I won a bursary to a famous grammar school, my mother had to work overtime to pay for my uniform and text books. I wasn't happy at the grammar school. It was too posh and I didn't fit. Most of the pupils were paying fees but a small handful of us, a required quota, were allowed in free. They did not make us welcome and they made it obvious that great things were not expected of us. I made friends, of course. The boys were not as hostile as their parents. I was always ashamed when I went to their homes. Somehow or other, if we invited them to ours, they had too much homework, or so their mothers said.

One boy's father was a banker. I will never forget the shame I felt when he gave me a lesson on proper table manners. I ate my pancake with a knife and fork and this disgusted him. When he asked what my father did, it was so they could 'fix' me on some social ladder. I said my father had died at the battle of Dunkirk and I glared into his face fiercely. He bowed his head and patted my arm. My roots in the slums had been forgiven. I had told a lie, of course.

Blood of All Colours
Because of the war, the masters at the grammar school were either medical rejects or retired old men called back to the desk. There was also a sprinkling of women. I could not judge their skills. The work was hard going. No one in my family could help with my homework. Oh, no, I wouldn't want to give you the impression that I was some woeful little waif from a novel by Charles Dickens. I am upset when I look back but I was quite oblivious at the time. There was bigotry but it didn't hit me till much later. I got my first thrashing for having a fight with a snob.

"Why did you hit him?" the Head asked sternly

"Because he hit me."

"Why did he hit you?" he probed.

"He said his father was a knight."

"So he is."

"I said he was called surplice or nightshirt."[6]

Without a flicker of a smile, he gave six 'easy' thwacks and put

---

6. A surplice is the white vestment worn by choirboys. "Nightshirt" was a nickname for someone who dealt in the black market.

me down for the school boxing team.

The Head quite liked me as a scholar and had some sympathy for my quandary. During the last year, we all had a chat about our careers. I told him that I wanted to study medicine and he advised me, quietly, that I came from the wrong background. I would need money and sponsors. I felt as if I'd been struck by lightning but I managed to keep a blank face. He said he would write to a firm of auditors on my behalf. I must add that in those days men who did accounts were looked on as little better than clerks. It was not even a trade because they just worked for you!

That July I got the best exam results in that or many previous years. I went along to the auditor. By one of those odd strokes of luck, which get less curious the more you think about them, he had been briefed by my father. I would work for him, apply to do my National Service early, and pick up an academic career later.

"Will I get in?" I asked.

"Without any doubt," he laughed. "And you can have your revenge on your old Head. Go to his old college and write him a letter of thanks - on headed notepaper! "

I would have been a rotten auditor and I feel that wealth can so easily lead to spiritual misery. If we ask everyone in society "What is enough?", their answers will have a direct link with their income. If we pass it all through a computer it would boil down to the same thing. "Enough is ... more than I've got now!"

3

APIS

The bull-god who gives strength to Pharaoh

Dying Embers

It seems so clear to me. I read a very urgent message and I feel my father in person talking directly to me. To my own eyes, it is explicit and clear. Our dreams are important if only because they comprise the star by whose light we steer our soul-boat through life. For some, hunger makes them seek satiety. Others, tired of being the underdog, search for power. But many men are driven by lust - and the quest for sexual conquest. What shall our children be like if they go on dreaming of mutant turtles or some electronic heaven far from reality?

"And who spins these dreams?" asked Crowley. "Who weaves the web that snares our imagination? Who would gain by draining our innate magical power? The answer, of course, is the forces of chaos. Powers who have copious cunning, enough to rollick in grease paint and perform the lesser roles - the ones least likely to catch the eye. They love the status quo because it's the next best thing to inertia."

His eyes blazed as he approached some sort of climax. "Jerusalem stinks of car fumes and pizzas. Xanadu bottles its own fizzy drinks. In the shadows of palaces there are cardboard cities where live fallen angels, cloaked in old sacks and aureoles of gin."

His mind made one of those dizzy leaps. "Would you know a demon if you saw one?"

I won't tell you what I answered. Instead, let me put the same question to you: can you recognize evil? In Oxford Street, the Champs Elysées or Broadway, are you clever at picking them out? How good is your vision among all those sparkling lights? How well can you hear things amid that gay, drunk laughter and tedious music? You don't go searching for green faces, forked

16

tails or horns, I bet! You realize that they'd be discreet.

Well then, how much less obvious are their minions going to be? Those men and women who do the devil's dirty work and try to seem as ordinary as possible. The human agents of evil resemble you and me. I accept, as I hope you do, that this makes it very awkward to present any proof. This, in its turn, makes it very easy for skeptics to scoff.

The question is then, do such things exist?

"Oh dear me, yes," said Aleister. "If people were not so stubborn, they'd see them all over the place."

He chuckled, but not with any great humour. "You don't have to be a Christian," he went on. "Judaism too has its devils. So does Islam! And so does almost every good religion in the world. They may not agree about God. They certainly don't agree about the proper manner of worship. But there is no argument whatever about the need to guard one's soul against evil."

As he mused for a moment, his mouth curled in a sly grin. "Funnily enough," he said, "the forces of evil feel more at home in the United States of America. It is obvious why, of course. In addition, there is a small particle of devilry in every bottle of ink, for example, and another that likes to house itself inside a set of traffic lights. But all in all, they find more openings on the other side of the Atlantic. Is it all due to refugees, I wonder? Their blood must be as pure as the scuppers of the Pequod."[1]

It was then that I asked one of the most important questions of all. "Where do they come from?"

He gazed at me so very intently I almost sensed the touch. "Why not follow one and see?"

"Is that what you did in Egypt, in Paris and all those other places?"

"Only once," he answered flatly, "in Morocco. All the other times, I ordered them to come to me."

Doctor Crowley

Shortly after we first met, he asked me quite casually, "What do you want to be when you grow up?"

"A doctor," I answered with no pause to think.

He hummed a moment like a sort of time-bomb. "And you have your bottles already, eh?"

1. The ship run by Captain Ahab in 'Moby Dick', by Herman Melville.

My mother had been talking. It was quite true though. My uncle had put up some shelves for me in an unused cupboard that was built-in to the wall. I used an old sheet as a curtain. It was my 'pharmacy'. In my eyes it was polished mahogany and tall, cut-glass bottles that contained mystic liquids that were as red as blood or as blue as a peacock's tail. I had made labels for each of them, copying the Latin phrases from a book I'd bought for sixpence in the old market. There was *Mist Tuss* or cough mixture and *Tinc Op et Cret* for diarrhoea.

"Why do you want to be a doctor?" my father went on. "Do you want to heal people? Or do you want to be a rich and important man?"

"Are doctors rich?" I asked in surprise.

"Very few starve to death," he chuckled, "and I've never seen one with bow-legs.[2] They take an oath and become gentlemen. But the first thing they do when they qualify is get their bills printed."

But my dream was such a tenuous dream and hadn't yet grown into anything more advanced. I blended skin creams and a herbal remedy for spots. I used to thrust them on people. If they didn't want to buy, they got them free. It wasn't the profit that interested me, it was seeing a good result. That's how I first got to know my grandma's friend, called Lizzie. They would often go to a pub with another room - the parlour, of course. To all intents and purposes it was part of the private house where the owner lived.

This was how the ladies kept their good name. They hadn't gone into the pub, you see, they'd been visiting the landlord's wife! It was all quite decent, they would explain. It would have been anyway, of course. But it was 'looks' that counted and, beside, the beer had such a good flavour when their excuse was proof against scandal.

On rare occasions, the people of the pub would organize a little trip in a bus.[3] They might go to a beauty-spot, such as Bolton

2. Rickets, or rachitis to give it its clinical name, is a softening of the long bones in growing children caused by lack of vitamin D. It occurred less and less during my childhood, but had been very common among the poor. There were many adults who had been stunted by the disease. Their legs bowed outwards almost in semi-circles, and their height was much reduced.

3. The regulars of a certain pub would save up, so much per week, and then organize an outing to an unknown destination on a bus. They usually went to a 'nice spot' for a 'nice tea', and then stopped for a couple of hours at a 'nice pub'. It was one of life's little highlights in those days. The now famous fish-and-chip shop, Harry Ramsden's, owes a lot to such outings.

18

Abbey, or even a show at a theatre. But coming back took much longer than going. They kept stopping for drinks, for pees, for fish-and-chips, and for police to transport someone they'd left at an earlier halt. During the whole journey home they all sang songs off-key. Very little was seen of them the following day. There wasn't one under the age of sixty. Each night of mischief needed a day to sleep it off.

If my grandma and Lizzie planned to go on such an excursion, they had to find someone who would "sit with Carrie". Carrie was Lizzie's elder sister and she was stricken with cancer. As often as not, they cajoled me into taking the job on. I could always do some homework, as long as I remembered to give her the medicine at intervals of one hour. They would leave it all ready: a row of egg-cups, each containing two tiny morphine tablets.

"I've seen to her," Lizzie would say, meaning she had changed her soiled sheets. "She'll be all right till we get back." But there was nothing they could do about that heavy, cloying smell. That was the stink of death being held at bay.

Poor Carrie! Her yellow skin, her big dog-like eyes, and her little moans and gasps of pain. "I'm bad," she would say every five minutes. "You'd better give me two of those egg-cups." I'd been warned that she would say this. She did it with any stranger - try to get them to help her commit suicide. I was such a prig, such an obedient lad! I would read her a book, praying that she'd fall asleep. Or I'd tell her something interesting about history, or physics. It was all beyond her ken. She did not understand a word. I was striving to take her mind off the pain and she knew. I stopped her pleading at least, and I gave her each dose of medicine at the due time.

But I also knew she was biting her tongue and hiding the tablets under the sheets. I noticed it, and I never said anything about it. Not a word. Not a comment. I went along with her little game. She was an old lady and I was a schoolboy. I had no right to tell what she should, or should not do. It was her pain, and her life. Somehow, it didn't feel quite natural to spoil things for her.

When grandma and Lizzie got home, Carrie was in a coma. It took them a minute or two to realize that she wasn't just asleep, and then it was all panic. Lizzie ran down the street to use the

19

public telephone box. My grandma sat at Carrie's bed-side and kept on patting her hand.

"It wasn't your fault," she said to me in case I felt guilty. She was feeling pretty bad herself. She then took hold of my hand and started squeezing it like dough. When the doctor came, he took a quick glance at me and then examined his patient. She died a few minutes later as we were all standing there. He put his arm round my shoulder and drew me aside as if we were going to talk man to man.

"You are a brave boy," he whispered, "much braver than me. You'd make a good doctor - if you could but keep your innocence."

I suppose many readers will think that he meant my sexual innocence or virginity. But this is not what he had in mind; he was alluding to my child-like simple and naive outlook. The sort of thing that lets a kid see the world in terms of 'goodies and baddies'. In the occult realm, as in the spiritual world in general, this is often alluded to as having 'clean eyes' or looking with 'eyes of wonder'. I didn't quite realize that he had guessed. Come to that, I didn't quite take in what it was he said. I felt a little bit like a criminal, but I was sure I had hidden all traces of my guilt. All I can think of now is the look of relief in Carrie's dead face.

The Soul Mirror
But Crowley had more in mind than that. "There are ways of taking illness away," he reminded me again. "You don't need to study anatomy or buy a wired skeleton." I wasn't sure what a wired skeleton was.

"It is the type of skeleton that medical students use. There is a special firm that reduces bodies to piles of bones, by boiling them, I believe. It then connects things together again by means of brass wire and rivets." He smiled grimly. "I've always thought that this would be a suitable end for many people in politics." He was to speak this way several times during the years that I knew him, and on each occasion he went further. He was giving me a slow and gentle briefing on some ancient mysteries which went back at least to ancient Egypt.

"If the tube-train system breaks down, do we mend it from the outside by pouring bottles of medicine down the steps of a station? No. We go inside. We discover the exact spot where something has gone wrong and put it right." He studied me for a few moments and took a deep breath. "The human being is a great many times more complex than the London underground."

It took several minutes for this to penetrate my mind and it was even longer before I started to understand what he might mean. As I looked up, he nodded. "Yes," he said. "You must go inside him." He could read my thoughts and he gave a little laugh. "No, not by the knife. Not even a light that burns.[4] But by the powers that course through you. You have a positive force that comes from being male, and you have a negative force that comes from being born of woman.[5] You must know him. You must love him. You must be one with him." Crowley gave a sudden shudder while he spoke, as if he were being directly seized by just such a force himself. He put out his hands and touched me on my puny chest and between my bony shoulders.

He did not squeeze me at all. He didn't apply any sort of pressure. Yet my breath seemed to freeze. My blood went thick and lazy. My heart seemed to open like one of those little fruit, a clementine, between his long fingers. It was as though I'd become a strange space-suit and he just stepped into me. Where my hands were, there too were his. His feet were my feet. I could hear his thoughts inside my head. The oddest thing was the way my age changed as if time's shuttle had begun to weave backward. I was both baby and man, child and pensioner, standing on the same threshold but waiting to both come and go. Time seemed to turn liquid. So did the physical part of my being. I was an upturned tool-box and each item that floated past my/his eyes would unfasten itself, like a regiment of soldiers who have been dismissed.

I felt clean. My soul felt polished. My physical being, my self, was put back together like a car engine that has been examined and checked out perfect. He let his hands fall. He looked haggard and very weary.

"At the age of two, when you were only a toddler, you trapped a finger in the cogs of your mother's wringer. You had one testicle that had not dropped and it was put right when you were five. When you were eight, your nose was broken during a fight

4. These words, spoken in the early 1940s, were a clear reference to the use of lasers.
5. This would be vice versa for a woman i.e., a negative force from being a woman, and a positive force from having been fathered by a man.

with a boy called Terence. Two years ago you had grave food poisoning after eating a Bombay Duck!"[6]

I was stunned as well as being a little unsteady on my feet. "How did you do that," I asked devoutly.

"Oh," he waved his hand, "like that. It's not too difficult once you've been taught. The only thing is, you must be prepared to let the illness come into yourself." He lifted his right hand to show me the crunched up index finger, dripping with blood. "You must just take my word about the testicle," he groaned and hobbled to his chair just in time to vomit.

I wanted to send for help but he stopped me. Over the next half hour, he became quite normal again and poured himself a large glass of whisky. "There are many ways of healing people but that is the best. In any case, all the others are derived from it." He lay back his head and let himself relax. "We call it - *The Elijah Method.*"

He was fast asleep and while he snored, I cleaned the place up.

6. I had got the name wrong. It was something called a faggot and it was made from breadcrumbs, herbs and minced offal. During the war we ate what we could get, and this had not been very fresh. He could only give it the name he found in my memory.

4
MEEYUTY

A god with a cat's head who guards a gate of the underworld

Pain and Fame

Perhaps this incident was at the back of my mind when I dreamed of being a doctor. Oh yes, I'm sure the memory stayed with me. I had been in hospital as a child. I had seen real doctors with my own eyes. How grand they were and how important they seemed. They were always dressed in shining white and they were moved about on castors by an adoring corps de ballet.

On the Junior Ward, the staff were usually kind, even a little bit indulgent, but all that changed when "the doctors' rounds" fell due. Sister became a Sergeant Major, barking at everyone as if we were late for a royal parade. Nurses ran, skidded, fell and sweated while one hid in the linen room and had an attack of hysteria. All the small patients were told not to move, not to speak and not to derange the bedding. We lay in two rows as stiff as pale corpses, and all watched with mounting nerves as the great man advanced toward our bed.

When he asked questions most of us were too paralysed to speak. "And how do you feel today," he would ask benignly.

"Oh he's coming along nicely," the sister would reply.

I doubt if he even noticed which person gave the answer - just so long as he got one. But I was quite determined to be brave. I wasn't a baby and I could speak for myself. The great judge looked at me over the top of some useless glasses. "Well now, Sunny Jim, did you move your bowels?"

"No sir," I denied hotly with a sense of outraged innocence. "It was him!" and I pointed to the lad in the next bed.

One nurse made a slight choking noise and went purple. But when the doctor smiled, the whole retinue relaxed and smiled too. "A right little comedian," the Sister remarked as they moved off, and she gave my big toe a ferocious twist.

In itself, this was a ritual. I had already seen several that had been performed by Crowley, so I felt that I knew one when I saw it. It was either a ritual - or a pantomime, and when you come to think of it, a pantomime is a kind of ritual too. The doctor played the principal role. They kept offering him sweets or apples, charts and clinical reports, or bottles of lemonade that looked very like holy water. He made a progress around all the aisles and between all the beds. Now and then he gave a special blessing with the magical rubber tube that dangled round his neck like a pectoral cross.

No matter where he walked, nor in which odd direction he turned, acolytes melted away before him, and those behind murmured a constant litany. He held the power of life or death in his hands. We all knew that. One could so easily take him for a stage magician putting on his act. None of us wanted to displease him, and I spent the rest of the morning wondering if his smile meant I would live ... and who had stolen those missing bowels.

I could quite easily picture myself being as important as that! But my main reason, however noble it sounds, was to stop people suffering. If needs be, I was even willing to share their pain.

"It can be done," said Crowley.

I looked at him sharply. I was not surprised that he had read my thoughts. I hadn't even twigged that he'd done so. It was his tone of voice, low and serious, that brought me up short.

"Nature creates pain as a warning. You are damaged. You are cut. You are in danger. The pain is supposed to prompt you into taking quick evasive action." We were looking at each other ever so steadily, and his message went deep and direct into my young soul. "Tread bare-foot on a drawing-pin and before you actually feel pain, you'll have flinched away to the opposite side of the room. The body can take crisis action quicker than the brain. And so, the pain is surplus." He paused and let that much sink in.

"The trouble with illness and disease is that the pain goes on after it's job has been done. We have answered the alarm and we are doing all the right things. But nature does not quite trust us. Like an Air Raid Warning - the siren will not stop sounding. We're all at full alert. Daggers of light carve the sky and ack-ack guns are shooting down the enemy. But she goes on with her

24

warning - and she'll go on and on with that warning until she gets the message that all is clear."

He looked at me with a piercing stare. "If all that fuss and howling is due to a dumb natural reflex, is it not proper that we should go higher and use mystical means? We must turn off the bells which frighten one so, and then attend to the cause."

Oh Cruel World

"We have the right to stop pain which is pointless. It is not done in order to hurt or punish. She wants you to survive and the anguish is just bad luck. She does not mean you to die from pain. As a matter of fact, nobody ever does."

He took hold of the thin muscle on my forearm and pinched it hard. "If it gets too intense, the brain blows a fuse and usually you faint." I snatched my arm away at once. It hurt like hell already. After all, Crowley was a big man and was not just playing with me. "The pain can stop," he said. "I order it to stop." He took hold of my arm and stroked it gently. "I will the darting energy in your nerves to slacken pace and to be calm. Let it be drawn toward me like pins toward a magnet. Let it stumble toward me like a blind puppy seeking warmth. Let the hurt withdraw from your body and enter mine. Like a house in the rain, let your pain drain to earth."

His eyes closed for a moment and I felt the pain fade away to nothing. I did wonder if this might be hypnosis, since that had been my subject for homework only the night before. Now he unloosed his cuff-links and pulled up his shirt sleeve. He held his arm toward me so that I could see quite clearly. At the precise spot where he had pinched me, his own flesh was bruised. The whole area was swollen and coloured with black, blue and green.

"To be able to do that," he said, rolling down his sleeve, "you must capture the meaning of love." There was a long pause and then he added: "Some men are even willing to die for love. I'm not talking about the doctrine of Redemption, nor do I refer just to Jesus Christ. I mean all men, in all times, who cared less for themselves than for the truth."

He leaned across and gave my hair one of those irksome ruffles that always annoy children. "Don't you be silly though. There have been enough futile gestures already." I'm still not sure exactly what he meant by that.

25

Bad luck does happen. It's normal that life should have its ups and downs. It makes things interesting. How weary a film would be, or a play in the theatre, if there were no tension. Would the sea be quite so alluring without the grandeur of its waves. Would the year inspire poets if it had no seasons? "Hope springs eternal in the human breast," said one poet.[1] "If winter comes, can spring be far behind?" replied the other.[2] It is the chords and arpeggios that catch the ear, and not the separate notes. So far as men are concerned, it is our emotional swings that give birth to a certain rhythm. Sometimes the pendulum in the soul is static, unmoving, but at other times it is like a metronome set for the gavotte.

There are hitches of course. Mishaps do happen from time to time. On the whole though, the system works and, in a manner of speaking, most of us frail humans look upon life as a binding contract. We can't quite remember when, but we feel that we have given our signature. We have a hunch, a feeling in our gut, that this is what we are supposed to be doing. It is not written in neon lights but - it seems right. Dogs should be dogs. Trees should be trees. Men should rise with the dawn, welcome the sun, and spend another day dying, while learning how to live. The only other choice is to learn nothing, but spend your days dying trying urgently to forget. On that route there is a large array of exits. One way is alcohol, drugs, a gas oven or nasty things ingested. A second way is duck ponds, church towers, railway tracks or the force of gravity. A third way is derring-do, shouting "down with France", "up the Pope", or winking at a man with a certain smile. We could be happy here. Why then do we quit the Garden of Eden and opt for the knacker's yard?

Privilege
If we leave aside prisons, padded cells and stately homes, there does seem to be order and routine in the world. In its turn, this implies rules, a being who makes rules, and a system of reward and punishment. To put it simply: everyone gets his fair share of meat and gristle, but whether he drinks Chablis or plain tap-water is a question that hangs on rank. That is outside the book of rules and you take it or leave it. But when the rules stop working, it is high time to worry.

1. Alexander Pope. 'An Essay on Man', 1753.
2. Percy Bysshe Shelley. 'Ode to the West Wind', 1819.

Persons like that, do they ever question their amazing good luck? Or does that sort of thing never enter their head? Do they take luxury for granted, like the Divine Right of Kings? Then what about those who have terribly bad luck? Oh yes, people who suffer certainly ask for reasons. "Why does God do this to me? Why is He so unfair? What have I done to deserve it?" they whine. Their plaintive wail does nothing at all to help their distress, but it may do something to relieve a bit of their anguish. It just crosses my mind to wonder if Princess Stephanie or Baroness Rothschild ever ask themselves that same question though: "What have I done to deserve all this?" I mean, everyone else in Europe knows! Don't we?

The Skin of my Teeth

But me too, I've done nothing. I've sung no bad songs. I have not told my social inferiors how to slide tainted fish into the flunkey's pocket. So why have I been the target for several attempts on my life? Now that I have said it, I can guess what the common reaction will be. *"This guy's bath has wheels on it!"* or *"This man's wig is nailed on too tight."* In short, you might think I'm mad. Well, before you call an ambulance, let me tell you about one or two of the incidents. I do have to tell you, of course, in case you should think that I'm lying.

First, they are not obvious. Arrows do not go zinging past my head in cafés. The chap behind doesn't get shot when I bend to tie my shoe-lace. Though I will admit that I still cross the street to avoid men with umbrellas! 'They' on the other hand are obliged to be subtle. Whatever else they do, they must not draw attention to me or to themselves. Then, if they fail to get me, as they always have done so far, there is no evidence left behind which I can brandish before the public eye. The result is that when I talk about this kind of thing, I can see the company's eyes cloud. It all sounds quite feasible, of course - and I do tell it so well but ... there is that elusive smell of paranoia in the air.

Instead of mounting a direct attack, they are cunning enough to use other events because - they're not too hot at magic. I can usually protect myself but, to visit England or anywhere else, I must use some form of transport. I cannot just beam myself down, like Captain Kirk. There are rules on that sort of thing. So I use cars, trains, buses, aircraft and ships.

I was booked to travel on *The Herald of Free Enterprise*. My enemies had foreseen the disaster but were five hours adrift with their figures. Pure chance? But of course. It is just such twists of fortune that they are able to utilise. Nowadays I always change my plans at the last minute. If you have been stranded in Dover, Plymouth or Heathrow - by strikes, by technical hitches, or even by flocks of sea-birds - you may have me to thank. Sorry!

About twenty years ago, some students invited me to speak at a meeting in a college in the midlands, and a friend offered to drive me down there at the weekend. To avoid the heavy traffic on the main roads, we took a detour across open country. The driver was chatting away quite merrily, and I remarked how dark it was getting all of a sudden. "Perhaps we're in for a storm," he said.

"One that appears out of nowhere?" I answered, and I had a funny, creepy feeling in the pit of my stomach. "Turn right," I said abruptly. For once my voice must have carried a tone of authority because he was shocked into action and did precisely as he was told. The car climbed a steep hill, and as we levelled out, we looked back down into the valley.

It was raining heavily on the road we had been following. Fifty yards further on from where we had left, there was a sharp S-bend that went straight across a hump-back bridge. Around that bridge, for about fifteen yards in each direction there was a patch of dense mist. The darkness was deepened by a single cloud that lay across the sun. Then, as the mist lifted, we saw that a car towing a caravan had got stuck on the bridge, the trailer was wedged between the two walls. We looked at each other and gulped. If we had gone our merry way, as planned, we would almost certainly have hit the back of the caravan!

Target for Tonight?
Whenever I visit England to see my various groups of students, I often stay at the same hotel in London. Four times out of five the fire-alarm goes off at two a.m. on Saturday morning and we are all ushered out into the street! It does not happen when I'm not there. Neither do the lifts break down when I'm not there. But I have to take it seriously. I have an uncanny feeling that if I stayed snuggled up in bed the fire would prove real.

If you are still not convinced, try another story. During one of these visits to London I had an afternoon free for shopping, so I took a bus for Harrods. But instead of turning down Brompton Road, the bus went on in the direction of the Albert Hall. In my hurry I had misread the number. I got off quickly and took a short cut towards Harrods. I came out of the little passage to find all traffic blocked, smoke billowing along the street, and red-cross trucks honking all around. It was the year of that infamous bomb explosion on the ground-floor. I missed it by approximately seven minutes.

I was passing Marks and Spencers in Paris, just opposite Les Galeries Lafayette, but instead of entering, I read the cardboard held by a young man sitting on the steps. "Out of work for two years," he had written in coloured crayon. "I am twenty-seven. I have a wife and two children." I was unkindly careful, since the Metro teemed with Gipsy kids, faces scarred with running sores, who pestered any person for money. You have to harden your heart a little or you'll end up poorer than them. But there was something about this young man which convinced me. He was cold. He looked starved. There was an empty, desolate look in his eye. I bent down to toss some money in his lap.

That is when one more bomb went off inside the shop. We both backed away in shock. I picked up his money for him but he ran away and left me holding it. It crossed my mind afterward - was he perhaps the look-out for the chap who planted the thing?

5

QADESH

The goddess of sacred ecstasy and sexual pleasure

Tunnels and Boxing

I have been accosted by a drab in Oxford Street who accused me loudly of rape. I have been knocked to the ground outside a bank by robbers beetling for their get-away cars. I have just gone into, or just left, stations where trains have crashed into the bumpers. I have stopped to buy an ice-cream just as a Taxi mounted the pavement a couple of yards ahead of me. I have gone into the Atlantis Bookshop[1], in Museum Street, London, when the shelves tipped over. I have been between two groups of youths when one decided to wipe out the other.

I would like to think that all these things are pure accident, but figures are against me. Someone or something is making use of random events to try and get at me. You are not convinced? Once, when I meant to buy a computer program, the shop which offered the cheapest prices had moved two miles up the road. When I found it at last, a friendly Aussie offered me a lift back.

We discussed the computer program, of course, and everything seemed quite normal. But as he slowed down to let me off near Marble Arch, a sort of change came over him. He grinned like Crocodile Dundee and said "Cheers mate." Then his face went blank and his voice went flat. "It's Aleister, right?" Well, it wasn't Aleister, but what a strange thing to say. He gave an empty grin as he pulled the door shut. Then, without a glance in his mirror, he drove straight across the road. He went over the central island and ploughed into the side of a Post Office van.

No, no, that's still not enough, but let me go on. How many people do you know who find live, giant spiders inside a bunch of

---

1. In 1972, I gave a plaque to the lady who ran the shop as a token of thanks. She had been kind enough to take copies of 'Liber Lucis' to sell, a duplicated publication put out by my students. Atlantis has survived many attempts at demolition.

bananas? Up to date, I've found six. Laurel and Hardy films excepted, is anyone ever hit by tins of paint dropping from a scaffold? I have seen two persons badly injured, and one killed. I go to a cinema and see sprawled legs and an open umbrella a little further on. If I'd tripped over one, I'd have been pierced by the other. While looking for an address in the old quarter of Cologne, the side of a house collapses some ten yards in front of me. I have drawn off the motorway to stop for a pee, and missed a multiple accident by seconds.

On the back-roads, going from Stonehenge to Exeter, I have stopped for a cup of coffee at a stall in a lay-by. As I drove away again, a caravan pulled in to take my parking place. Then the gas cylinder for its little stove exploded. I receive telephone calls from 'my' broken hearted wife, who sobs and begs me to think of our children ... or from husbands who beg me to let their wives go free. At various times, while staying with friends, there have been sudden deliveries of cement, gravel, farmyard manure or even a flock of sheep.

Once, I received a telephone call from a local newspaper which wanted to check the facts for my obituary.

Before you start pointing it out to me, let me tell you that I have already noticed it myself: in a certain way, most of these things seem like bad jokes. They are childish, absurd, ludicrous and potty. Quite! So that when I list them, you are more likely to doubt my state of mind than the reality of these events. But they do go on happening, and they are latently dangerous. I'm not going to let them succeed just to show you I'm right. If I am daft, I'm not as daft as all that!

If I wanted to make up stories like these, I'd be a great deal more lurid and fanciful. Somehow or other, they're not quite as dramatic as they should be. I think I know why. By leaving room for other interpretations, the person or persons responsible make it that bit more difficult to convince others that I'm telling the truth.

I could have weeded out the petty stuff and the minor detail. I could have doctored the record and focussed on the big stories which are more likely to catch your eye. That's what I was going to do. That's how I decided to play it. But then a voice told me that if I start *editing* the truth, it wouldn't really be the truth any more.

I'm glad to say that I can still tell flights of fancy from the everyday trivia of life. In my own opinion, all this weird stuff is just a cheap way of giving me a warning. But how would you feel, if someone sent you a packet with a pair of joke glasses inside - the kind with macabre eyeballs on shaking metal springs. Can you imagine? Would you just have a good laugh? But you'd stop laughing the next day, when some young kid is tossed off his bike by a puncture - and the handle of his brakes gets embedded in his face!

So far, I have escaped all of these traps. The results have been dreadful for others, but all they did to me was cause a minor upset to my plans. If you remember, I told you I was a psychologist, so I do know what paranoia is. I know how it must sound then when I recount all these things. But I still go ahead and do it. If they were delusions (and I promise you that such things are quite possible to do by magic) I would never have mentioned them. Perhaps I have roused your curiosity? Well don't invite me to join you in a Chinese meal or else your noodles might start moving, and your chopsticks dangle limp wool between your fingers.

I don't mind telling you though. That's the point to grab. I know who is behind it, you see. It's really quite simple, and if you tried, you could work it for yourself. Let me give you a tiny hint: instead of worrying about "who?", start asking yourself the other question - "why?".

As far as I'm concerned, it is either some of Hiram's boys[2], flown in specially from Jerusalem no doubt, or else it's someone with a slight German accent. But then again, it could simply be some of their camp followers, who believe they are working magic. I doubt if government agents could pull it off, though these days, you can never be sure. No! I have my own ideas on the subject, and I am going to start using the principle of ricochet or boomerang magic.

Talking at Cross Purposes

"Bash the Bishop" was Crowley's term for the act of sexual self-relief. I don't for one moment believe that he coined such a phrase himself. Probably it dated back to one of the public schools he'd

---

2. Hiram is the supposed Egyptian architect who designed the Temple of Solomon - and the mythical founder of Freemasonry.

attended and it exhibits once again his total disregard for the church.

Being one of your average slum-kids, I had never met a bishop myself. I wasn't at all clear what it was. At Sunday School they once said the bishop was coming on a diocesan visit. I thought we might be having injections so I didn't go. The only other bishop I came across was a certain Geoffrey Bishop who was good at football. And that was it! So when Crowley talked about bashing the bishop, I was all at sea and had no idea what he meant. True, he was a chess fanatic but ... ?

"The Bishop wears a mitre," he explained with great patience, "and often a cowl. If you fawn on him, chuckle[3] his chin, and comfort him, he puffs up amiably with inspired pride. Give his crozier a rub and out pops a smiling genie, ready to make your wildest dreams come true."

I asked the question that mattered most to me, "What's a mitre?"

There was a sharp intake of breath and he regarded me with a glassy eye. "Do you butter the wrong side of your bread, by any strange fortune?"

"Is there a wrong side?" I mused like a young Hamlet.

"Of course," said he, quaking like a turkey, "the backside!"

The penny dropped and to his obvious relief I burst into loud peals of laughter. It was if a great weight had fallen from his shoulders.

"I didn't like to ask," he mumbled, "but being brought up by two women ..."

He had nothing to worry about on that score. If I was slow to catch his meaning, I had been ahead of everyone else in terms of physical growth. I had not understood him because we had a whole new jargon now, and his terms had sunk with the Ark.

At my school, you could ask a boy "Can you shoot yet?" If he was in the know, the correct answer was "You should see my gun!" If he was too young, too innocent, no great harm was done. The 'newcomers' (think about it!) would line-up behind the bicycle sheds and, facing downhill, they would have a competition to see who could 'shoot' the farthest. The older boys even placed bets.

Doing it before a witness was called 'losing one's cherry', while

3. This seems to be one of AC's neologisms. He used it more than once.

33

doing it with someone else was called 'Thomas à Beckett' i.e. laying hands on a Bishop! The secret language may or may not have been necessary, since the teachers were all too old for the army or else medical rejects. Yes, we had filthy minds and we did the foulest things you could imagine. So we grew up normally in spite of the adult intrigue to turn us into stainless angels.

"We each put a penny in the kitty," I told Crowley. A penny was a lot of money in those days! "Whoever gets there first wins the lot and wears a tin-badge that says 'The Fastest Gun in the West'."

My father roared with joy and dabbed away his tears. "And I dare say that you are the champion, eh?"

"Well," I faltered, "I would be if it wasn't for the twins. Their dad owns a big restaurant and they eat better than me."

"That's not fair," he cried. "That's cheating and it's illegal and it's part of the black market." He stopped dead, eyes blazing. "I shall write to a friend in Bradford," he snorted. "You'll eat bacon and eggs for breakfast. You'll have fillet steak for lunch. You won't much like it but you'll have a raw egg in Guinness every night. You're on a new diet, my lad."

I do not claim to be an expert on nutrition. But I am over six feet tall. I am built like a rugby back. My furnace is still stoked high. Many people say I am the spitting image of my father. Perhaps the steak had some magic in it?

Once the ice was broken, Crowley felt able to discuss such things more openly. However you may judge his sexual leanings, he always behaved properly about what he did or didn't say to me. Once the topic was broached, he was not so much evil as totally free of guilt and quite unabashed. Apropos the topic of manual thrills, "One can't sing Handel's 'Messiah' solo," he said, "but one might, during rehearsal!"

There was a secret grin on his lips and I knew he was telling me something that was crucial to his system of magic. "God alone knows when the next Olympic Games will be[4] but all the would-be entrants are training like mad. One does not notice them much. The reason being that they don't throw the shot, do long-jumps down the High Street, or run the Marathon when the buses are late. They work their ankles, they stretch their backs, they keep their muscles in trim. They get themselves ready for

4. The International Olympic Committee had suspended them for the duration of the war.

the big day by striving for a little progress each and every day."

Our Good Humour

He ruffled my hair, which always upset me. I do it myself now to others and I can see it irritates them. But one is not doing it for fun. Neither is one giving the roots a massage or trying to clean the scalp. Under the guise of a tender gesture, one is sending a little boost to the soul's batteries.

"To make progress in magic, one must not be afraid to try unusual things. To go up into the big boys' college, one must know the correct way of invoking power." His lips twitched and I knew that a joke was coming. "You will feel such an imbecile if you go off at half-cock, so to speak!"

I giggled to oblige him but what was half-cock? "Are there wrong ways then?" He knew damn well that I was playing him along.

"Well, of course!" he said. "You wouldn't use sandpaper."

I hooted with laughter and he was quite chuffed to have scored a point so readily.

"The whole subject is comic to young lads who are still bashful. But you must also think of it as a magical act." He grew serious. He knew just how to work such changes. He could slide in a joke when he was profound, and instil a touch of pathos into your hilarity.

"To be a happy man you must conquer sex, rather than let it dominate you. Do not approach your penis as if it were a noxious slug but use it like a lightning rod. If you are going to do it anyway, then do it lustily or else it can be dangerous."

I thought about this for a few moments, and then I said: "The sports master says it can make you blind."

"Is that why his wife left him for another man?" For a split second, I saw outrage in his eye. "Even you children can draw down the dragon's breath, the original creative forces that support the cosmos. How myopic to avoid it. How much better to direct the flow into good channels. That is why even the simple, solo act should be earnest and flagrant."

I can't pretend that I was innocent, but try as I might, I couldn't see how a simple wank could be either earnest or flagrant. I listened to him closely and he knew that he had my full attention. He was always careful not to shock my naivety or tell

35

me too much, too soon. He tested the ground in his own refined way. He just dropped his own terms and tried to adopt our current ones.

"How do you stand as regards clay-pigeons?" He asked out of the blue.

"With my legs open and torso locked!"

I had replied to the literal question itself where he had been using my own school jargon for sex. He roared with laughter. He just bent double and chortled. It soon dawned on me that I had made a good joke by accident, though he gave me full credit for being a great wit.

"How do you stand on income tax?" he hooted. "With my legs open! Ho, ho, ho!" He slapped his thigh. "How do you stand on the Church of England? Hee, hee, hee - with my torso braced!"

I laughed with him for a while. Each pushed the other closer to hysteria. But he went on too long and hearing a remote wheeze of asthma, I tried calming him down. It crossed my mind that he may have taken a drink or two. To my surprise he brought out the decanter at once. He had read my mind.

Sex-magic came up as often as anything else. If anybody wanted, they could easily twist what I say. Hence I must make it quite clear that Crowley did not dwell on sex in an unhealthy fashion. I am pulling things out of a rag-bag of memory. I'm picking out words and phrases from here, there and everywhere. In order to make my point, I am the one erecting the case.

He believed that most people had already been sabotaged by the time they were twelve. But for that, there would be little need to raise the subject.

At another time he said: "Like food, sex is there to be enjoyed. But you will not find God by stuffing yourself ... or anyone else, for that matter!"

He also made it clear that in his opinion, a lot of mental illness had been caused by the church's attitude toward sex. Giving priests the benefit of the doubt, he said even were they sincere, they still created evil in God's name.

"After what you have no doubt heard on Sundays," he said, "you will be surprised to learn that Satan has little interest in sex and no special sweet tooth for virgins! We have simply clothed him in our own fears and dreams." He waved his hands in a theatrical gesture. "All of which makes life hell for the trainee magician."

On another occasion he expressed it this way. "Since sex is going to happen anyway, why not use it in a good cause and make it count? Why waste it all on going mad when it could be used for healing and such?"

So far as this concerns me in person, I can only say: Point taken, papa.

6

TAYET

The goddess who makes the cloth for binding mummies

An Astral Timetable

AC kept a 'magical diary' which was guarded by his old friend and former student, Mr Gerald Yorke. It now rests, along with other archives, in the Warburg Institute, London.

In his diary, Crowley made cryptic remarks to remind himself of what he had done, where he had done it, and when. Some authors assume that they have 'cracked his code', so to speak, and that they can therefore read his diaries as clearly as a railway timetable. This is not quite the case. Let us say rather that they see what they expect to see. However, according to AC, keeping such a magic diary is essential if one is aiming to build a head of steam in order to start a certain engine moving. Or to put it in other words, it is a necessary opening to certain kinds of magic and ritual.

The theory behind the praxis is extremely complex and, even though he spelled it out for me, it took many years for me to grasp it clearly. Certainly it would be far too ambitious to try and cover the topic here. In brief, one part is a type of normal routine and is designed to aid the daily renewal of self and one's internal energies. But a second part, less obvious, is reserved for '*high days and holy days*'. This is all about the application of magic to one's intentions in this world. It goes without saying that Aleister did not keep a diary merely to have something hot to read on the train!

The principles behind sex magic are not in the least depraved. Unlike roses, bottles of bubbly, or a brace of etchings, sex magic contains nothing which is designed to help one seduce potential but unwilling partners. It has nothing to do with bending people to your will, or of beating their personal morality. True, one can get rid of the ballyhoo and the artifice - get down to brass tacks, so to speak ... but the basic aim is to be a better *conduit* for a stronger flow of cosmic forces. If only the world were not so prudish, we could liken sex magic to a form of therapy ... but a highly unusual one, inasmuch as *it works*!

My own approach to this subject is to relate the rhythms inside us to those that govern the earth, e.g., via the phases of the moon. On the continent, gardening books or news reports will talk about the moon's phases as a guide for sowing and planting. Yet science assumes that no other factor but temperature gives the necessary signal for buds to sprout and fruit to grow.

If one is a cattle farmer, one should keep a register of the dates on which cows were served, and the ensuing dates of calving. If one then superimposes the details about the moon's waxing and waning, then the connection hits you with the force of a karate kick. Using this kind of knowledge, plus a little magic, I have helped many infertile couples to become happy parents of quite healthy kids.

Crowley was over the top at times. He flung back the doors of perception and let the dreams flow freely. He could do this easily because of his harsh childhood in the house of Christian bigots. At that time, in Britain, it was widely believed by doctors and laymen alike, that 'self-abuse' was the main cause of syphilis, insanity, loss of teeth, and "putrid refluxes from the brain".

When I asked him his opinion on all this, he simply replied: "Strange place to keep your brain, what?"

Human Growth Agenda

Children haven't got any sexual desire.

When they go to the cinema, it is to watch Tarzan or Indiana Jones. What they are looking for is exciting battles, narrow escapes, secret codes, hidden treasures and traps. They want a world that is neatly divided into goodies and baddies. You can imagine their fury then when the screen switches to drooling kisses, seduction and sloppy stuff like that. You must have heard them - the howls of derision from the front row. Children's film producers know only too well what the rules are. The hero has only to glance in a girl's direction and the young audience will fight, fetch ice-cream, go for a pee ... or all three things at once!

Those who set out to amuse children must not take needless

risks or they will lose their audience! Children select their heroes with very great care. They feel terribly let-down if these heroes do not conform to their own (the children's) proper code of honour. From Hereward the Wake, to the latest thing in spacemen: he-men rescue women but they do not stop to have a touch. They get out quick to look for other dragons!

Now I wonder if you have noticed how modern underwear has been getting more and more like the weaponry of war - with bras like tin helmets and men's knickers like catapults! Once one has passed safely beyond infancy, and nappies are things of the past, then underwear performs much the same function. They are meant to be 'discreet linings' which can be lifted out and washed as necessary. Their basic and original purpose was to stop your natural bodily filth from soiling your very much more expensive outer clothes.

But the way Nature has fashioned us, those parts of the body that we use for the one purpose, are also used for another one. This does not become apparent until you have passed a certain age and the penny has dropped. Then, all at once, underwear becomes a subject of fearful shyness and of burning glamour. These flimsy garments seem to mutate overnight into a kind of global code system between men and women. Instead of passing by, like ships in the night, lonely souls can now send signals. They give out little flashes of inviting light: warm heart open to offers again.

The weird thing is that from this moment on, underwear becomes high fashion. One spends enormous amounts of money on it because it is meant to be seen. Now we hit on a rather delicate point. If one is undressing in the presence of the opposite sex, then *one is likely to be going all the way*. This means that men do not buy costly underwear in order to attract women. They wear it where it will be noticed by other men - in the sports hall, the swimming pool or a changing room. This is how they can brag safely. Male underwear is meant to show off in a way that only other men appreciate! (Did you know that, on the continent, one can buy the male equivalent of 'falsies'!)

Little lads prefer airplanes to women. They think that older folk are ill. As Crowley told me: "One can have no sympathy for an emotion one has not felt!" So when elder brothers moon round the house, showing all the symptoms of lead poisoning, younger kids imagine they must have been whacked on the head. I used to think that love was a type of measles.

But if sex is unknown, every boy in the world goes to sleep hanging on to the bit that resembles the neck of a balloon. This is not any morbid fear of possible inflation, but just a nice, cosy sensation that gives him a feeling of great comfort. Some children may even do the same thing during the day.

Parents do their best to stop it, of course, especially if the vicar has dropped in for a cup of tea. Mind you, there are some vicars who would not be all that deeply offended! Be that as it may, so far as a little boy is concerned, his 'willie' performs very much the same function as a rabbit's foot or any other good-luck charm. For a brief period in his life, it becomes a kind of talisman that protects him from "things that go bump in the night".[1]

Then, all of a sudden, it turns into the good sword, Excalibur!

Church Obscenity

Crowley said that under the right conditions, almost anyone could muster an intense type of cosmic power. But it was crucial to know the ancient wisdom to be able to project that strength in the form of an invisible bolt which might complete a magical operation. "Anyone possessed of a penis should be obliged to lend it to the war effort," he declared like a despot. "And those who lack one should be closely searched to find out where they're hiding it!"

On another occasion, he told me that a man was a woman turned inside out. "Picture the mystic beast itself," he went on. "Male and Female coupled in a crimson crucible[2], back to back, like reversed jewels in an induction coil waiting to be hurled skyward like a sacred lance."[3]

He took me to visit an old, Saxon church, and showed me a bizarre carving.[4] It was a crude likeness of a woman using both hands to open her vagina. "You are not being invited to tea and scones" said Crowley. "She's telling you she could swallow you whole and, one inside another, you'd fit like old socks."

1. An anonymous prayer from Cornwall: From ghoulies and ghosties, and long leggedy beasties, and things that go bump in the night, Good Lord deliver us.
2. From Latin: crucibulum, meaning 'night light', and Arabic: kermes, meaning trisulphide of antimony. Crowley pointed to this combination as being the true origin of Rose Cross.
3. This, and other florid phrases that he used, were obvious references to certain alchemical processes, but not necessarily orthodox ones.
4. Known as Sheela-na-gigs or given a nickname such as Gipsy May.

As a child of the slums, I was also a puritan and his sporadic crudity was a way of smoothing corners and jolting my smugness. It wasn't that he had a foul mouth, but he never flinched from calling a spade a spade. "You should go to Autun,"[5] he said. "The cathedral has some nice obscene gargoyles and other carvings. One jaunty manikin seems ready to fart in the devil's face, and bugger him both in, and back to, the nether regions!"[6]

Nature ensures that a teenager's nervous system is ready for the first orgasmic trial but until then, like a puppy, he can only wag his tail. The internal clock will throw all the right switches at the right time and the boy will be sculpted into man. His first erection excites him and he soon finds ways of reaching an orgasm. The flame will never burn quite as strongly as now. For about a year or two, a young lad fingers himself with all the ardour of a budding flautist.

But if youth has the physical ability for sex, it is totally lacking in the field of social know-how. These are the years of burning loins and swollen hearts when love's true dream is smashed by shyness and shame. The skills are a long time in arriving. So many things have to change. He has to learn a new type of conduct, a whole set of new opinions, and most difficult of all - a new kind of morality.

The skin begins to alter and erupt in acne; the emotions change and cause a kind of passing madness. If this sticks - if they can't struggle out of it - then they grow into men with tangled thoughts and sexual problems. There are three quite clear signs. First, the person is ultra modest about his body. Second, there is a very marked reserve in his speech and his emotions. Third, he is very nervous on the subject of sex and may even display panic.

We are the only animal which can be crippled by its own thoughts. This is why the hunchback asked[7]: why was I not made of stone, like thee?" We are taught to feel such massive guilt and such intense remorse that we go on blaming ourselves for the rest of our lives. Our hearts are choked by unknown fears.

It is a very perilous stage in which normal men can be pushed toward deviant sex or even impotence. We have been saying it for

5. An ancient town in the French department of 'Saone et Loire'.
6. You may have to hurry because "restoration work" is under way and many figures are becoming "de-paganized" in the process i.e. they are somehow losing all their earthy vulgarity
7. Notre Dame of Paris, by Victor Hugo, 1831.

years, Aleister Crowley and I, and only recently have doctors started to agree[8] that *such grave conditions are not inborn but acquired.*

The basic problem is that while we are young, we are not prudent enough to see progress. As far as sexual pleasure is concerned, we go hunting for 'more'. We are so enslaved by the physical that our soul forgets that it has needs too. Inner vision is lost. The third eye is blinded. That hunger for *"just one more orgasm"* kills our higher potential.

"One cannot avoid sex," said Aleister Crowley. "One sinks, or else one learns to swim."

Signposts and Guides

Liberty, Equality and Fraternity - how lofty that sounds and how noble it looks when carved in stone. But the words are lies! No one is free, none are equal and we are forever killing our brothers from other countries or other creeds.

In England, the animal rights people kill babies in prams. In Ireland, the IRA kills anything that walks on two legs. In poor Cambodia they have killed until the very stones bleed. Mother Earth is like a grieving widow in weeds and little by little she is abandoning all hope. She is sinking to her knees. She is giving in. She is yielding before our eyes.

But we have no pity. We have no sense of imminent loss. There is even the possibility that we will reduce her to nothing with our own bare hands. That's right! We may yet kill Dame Nature. Do you know what happens when men try to kill gods? The skies crack. The Day of Doom comes down!

You can't hide from these things. It's no good strumming your harp while Rome burns. Rebels shout their slogans as they are being shot but they also soil their trousers. A heroic death? "From dust to dust", says the Prayer Book[9]. But was there a little something before and is there anything at all after? We only look at the sandwich itself, you see. We worry ourselves to death about those twin coatings of dust and we even waste the wonderful filling called life. Old Nick hasn't yet won, but he has not exactly lost, either!

There's a fork in the road a short distance ahead. Each of us

8. A letter in 'The Sunday Times', 22 Sept.1991
9. The rubric for The Burial of the Dead, as used in the Anglican church.

may go whichever way he wishes, but that is our only freedom. That is our one and only liberty. We may choose as we wish, but only between the two options: left path or right. Do we go where we would, or where we should? It doesn't seem much, this endowment that makes us human, but just a drop more would transform us.

What an awesome skill, to be able to change tracks and go in a different direction! We shuffle the cards and, by changing the draw, we alter world history. The question is though, are we playing at God! Are we usurping some divine mandate which makes the duty too heavy to be carried and drives us closer to madness? To be a pilgrim, you must be able to tell a hero from a hotspur.

Your opinion does not count in the least. What is, is! It appals me to see fools shaping truth out of scraps of their own experience. Today they call it New Age, but there's nothing new about it! Men were always misled by their emotions. In my grandma's day, Vesta Tilley[10] sang about it. "*A little of what you fancy does you good!*".

New Age is what Aleister called "A bit of a pig's breakfast! By which I mean a motley mash of inedible slops that they serve in Turkish prisons and one of the Oxford colleges."

There is no spiritual value in this occult stew. It may stave off hunger but it will not nourish nor enable you to grow. Like the hand-made 'jewelry' sold in the streets, it is only wire and beads. You are charmed by the 'artist' and it doesn't look too bad in the street lighting. I regret to say that truth is not for bending. *These men are not prophets.*

The most evocative sounds are not music but a baby's cry, a loving sigh, a soldier's moan in the mud. But New Age music has all the subtlety of a Hollywood film-score and the same mesmeric effect as gas at the Dentist's. It is mainly due to electronic chance and not to any kind of esoteric truth. This is not the voice of the Beyond so much as wishful thinking. They would gain a lot more inner light from the mystic sound of Placido Domingo trying to throttle one Luciano Pavarotti.

Pretty? Oh yes, it's pretty, but so is tinsel, candles on a birthday cake, and sparklers, but no one expects them to provide light. It's as fatuous as going for a romantic stroll down a cul-de-

10. A much loved star of the Victorian music-halls.

sac *from which you will have to come back!* Are you as dumb sheep waiting to be shorn? Do you go gladly on this wild goose chase? The state your minds are in, wobbling on the brink of a fearful neurosis, is it all just a holiday? Fine, fine, so you can dance the gavotte. But can you find your way through the maze?

7

TA-BITJET

The scorpion goddess who can cure poisonous bites

How it came about

Rudolf Steiner lived from 1861 until 1925. He left the arms of theosophy, and after a stint as Grand Master of the O.T.O. in Vienna, he founded his own group.[1] After World War I, Steiner brewed a blend of politics that echoed the slogan of the French Revolution. His vision was a mix of dynamic ideas from Theosophy, the O.T.O. and Manicheism. He probably got all this from my father who, as titular head of the O.T.O. in England, was present at many of the international meetings.

Sadly, Steiner was also interested in 'odd' things which have also become popular in the last thirty years. I have in mind the fad for organic food or curing everything by means of pretty crystals. But then there are the incense sticks, the plumb-bobs, the weird music, the 'art' and that cooky way of bringing up children. Thirty years from now, they'll be making films about you: The Lotus Eaters.

In part, he was spurred by the downfall of the 'Old Europe' with all its pre-war values. During the 1960s, though, a new kind of socialism began to evolve. This was partly due to the Vietnam War and partly to the wave of total boredom which swept through the western world. This tidal wave was able to take into itself, and quell, many opposing brands of extremism. This is now entitled *The New Age Movement*.

It has very little visible organization, its declared aims are "against the status quo", and it is the secret arm of a recreant group. I quite agree that it looks harmless. I can almost hear old ladies defending it, like a trembling, little doggy with limpid eyes. But mark my words, if you please: this little doggy bites, and its

---

1. He called it The Anthroposophical Society.

bite is dangerous.

Rock music was one expression of the new anarchy; drugs and sexual frankness was another. Magic and the occult were also part of the same vague yearning. The Beatles, don't forget, put Aleister Crowley's face on the cover of one of their most famous albums: *Sergeant Pepper's Lonely Hearts' Club Band*!

Many folk felt themselves lifted up and inspired by the coming of the so-called Age of Aquarius. It is all to do with "reigning signs of the zodiac", you see. According to the unfounded myth, the earth passes from the influence of one into that of another every two thousand years. There is lots of conjecture and very little mystic evidence. Myself, I'd put the idea in the same file as Jules Verne or Steven Spielberg, and call it creative thinking.

Those who believe in these things are very serious, but they find it difficult to pin down the year. I mean to say, what is the basis for our counting the years the way we do? The Islamic way of counting is unlike that of the Jews, and the Jewish way of counting is not like ours. The Chinese, who seem to do very little else, have been counting for much longer than most. Myself, I am not so for or against anything as to wish to rock the boat. If you like, we can start again tomorrow and let Year 1 begin.

But since the units of measure are devised by man, why should there be a grand machine in the sky which helpfully gears itself to our system? The last epoch was not the Age of Pisces unless you are a Christian. You can't both be an occultist and also think that cosmic events hang on the date of Jesus' birth! But it's no good being sensible in matters of faith.

The supposed switch from Pisces to Aquarius is overdue. I may as well tell you that it has already happened: it occurred the day that I myself was born.[2] This gives you a better idea of it's true significance, since nobody even noticed!

Let me summarize the facts:

1. the number 2,000 has no link with man's destiny.
2. occultism per se is not beholden to astrology.
3. the calendar and the zodiac are human constructs.

Fishers of Men & Fascists

This notion of an Age of Aquarius is very appealing but is not

---

2. Astrologers please note: in my first book I state quite clearly that I have changed all dates and biographical detail slightly! Please do not send me any sample horoscopes!

germane to magic or mysticism. The New Age movement found it too handy to ignore and decided to wear it like a limp cockade. Youth was gripped by the vision of a perfect society in which there were no more wars, famines, plagues or poor. The Horsemen of the Apocalypse would fall off their steeds and fragrant peace would rule the world. It is a rosy vision where youth is not crushed by broken dreams.

The hidden hand behind the New Age movement is not a Great White Community. It is a commercial network that makes and sells the bait, the lures and the dud candles that are the makings of a spiritual hot-pot. It looks like a joy-ride, a fun thing, a religion without rules. In fact, it very much savours of the Jazz Age - the carefree spree that marked the run-up to the Second World War. It is run, from a safe distance, by a group which aims to wrest political power and twist public opinion in Europe, Asia and the USA.

They timed it well. The church lost a whole generation just because the Pied Piper tootled a better tune. It was made from bits of things that seemed 'good' - Amnesty International, scraps of Greenpeace, Save Rabbits or anything else that switches people on. It is what we can call a utility creed, and intended to be a sort of occult Esperanto. There being no basic orthodoxy, it can be used to skim the cream off one's intellect.

Only evil could have caught the mercuric energies of youth as simply as this.

Oddly enough, many new factions claim to preserve and develop the teachings of the O.T.O., and a handful of them profess to follow AC's path.

The most recent neo-Templar group[3] was born (or let loose) in 1984. Its main principle is to get the world ready for the coming Aquarian Age. This it will do with the aid of ideas found among the original Templars. Where did they come across this material? Your guess is as good as mine. But I am pretty sure they got a secret message from Jacques de Molay.[4] Or they stumbled on an ancient manuscript in the attic of their grandma's house.

I need hardly remind you that the O.T.O. was founded by pan-German zealots with extreme right-wing views, between the years

---

3. "L'Ordre Internationale Chevalesque Tradition Solaire"
4. The last Grand Master, burned alive by Philip le Bel of France, in the early 14th Century.

1895 and 1900.[5]   One was called Karl Kellner and the other was Theodor Reuss.   Both were top rank Masons.   Many of these have political links, and most of them lean towards the far right. While enemies still do accuse Crowley of having been a magical fascist, he taught a form of spiritual freedom that was above politics and much closer to the Gnostic view.

As you might expect, the O.T.O. does not care to dwell on this.

The Importance of Being Earnest

Why should it be easy?   What do the Gods care if you live on lettuce, recycle sewage, or stand up for feminism? "Your concerns are not theirs", Aleister said when I got too proud. "You are no less loved than your enemies. The gods are above us, watching over the world, winding up the solar system, and shifting galaxies over the face of the cosmos. Don't ask if they are on your side. Wonder instead if you are on theirs!"

Learning to be humble was hard for a kid. It's harder still once you've grown up. We are so eager to defend an opinion that we don't even realize that it is only an opinion. Somehow or other, like a ship's hull that needs scraping, our mind can founder from heavy emotions. We don't just think, we feel - and because we feel, we start to believe.

"When zeal governs the brain," said Aleister, "and verdicts are made by emotion then, alas, one is trapped by the logic of a sea-side donkey!".

Do you have anything solid to go on? Did you get a message from beyond? You presume that the gods sent it, but have you checked? They're very busy, you know. Why would they pause in their work? And why you? Suppose for a moment it was not the gods and you've been listening to something other?

You would make sure, wouldn't you? I mean to say, you would not mislead other people or risk ruining the Plan just out of personal pride, would you? If you feel you have a warrant, then who gave you your orders? You are taking great risks, of course. You are gambling for very high stakes. But you have thought it over. You have pondered the matter. Because you don't want to

---

5.   The whole cavalcade was derived from something called "the Masonic Rites of Memphis and Mizraim". These have nothing to do with Elvis Presley, but were made by an English chap called John Yarker - a Freemason.

be like Lucifer, the "bearer of light", do you? Despite all the evidence, he goes on thinking that the gods are wrong, and he still believes he is right. You are not seeking a conflict. You're not a rebel, are you?

Can your faith explain the idea of wrong or evil? Crowley said[6] "Do what thou wilt is the whole of the Law" - but everything depends on how you analyse the phrase. You are not allowed to ignore those last two words: *The Law.* He is not telling you to do whatever you like because the formula goes on, you remember, "Love is The Law, Love under the Will."

You may very well argue that Crowley knew about Schopenhauer, Nietzsche and Fichte - but he also knew more than most about Gnosticism. You will notice that he does not specify your will, his will, or group will. He is clearly meaning *The Will,* or an aspect of the gnosis.[7]

Will is also the future tense of the verb, to be. "I am that I am" says God in the Bible.[8] Crowley read this meaning in the words: "*I will existence. Let being be.*"

But this doesn't concern the New Age people, does it? They think in terms of an earthly paradise here and now. So then, this is what it's all about - Scorpio and lung cancer, royal jelly and racism, meusli and cocaine, love and AIDS, tinkling temple bells and the bombing of cities! You belong to an old religion, mate! It's been around for thousands of years. It's called The Worship of Novelty.

Free-will

Let me quote Aleister Crowley again, "Pleasure is not the goal so much as the carrot that gets us there!" Today the world is pledged to the mass production of carrots and we are addicts, like Bugs Bunny. But unlike Bugs Bunny, we are falling blind. Other things can turn you on, but pleasure is more easily come by.

Without wishing to spoil it for you, pleasure does not always satisfy, and one can have too much of it anyway. Doctors say it can curdle your brain, priests say it poisons the soul, and a certain women's weekly says it's terrible for marriage. I say it hinders the quest and lets truth go to hell.

6. He wasn't the first! The idea goes back in time - not just to Rabelais - but to the Gnostics.
7. see: R.M.Grant, 'Gnosticism and Early Christianity', Harper Torchbooks, 1966.
8. Exodus, 3:14.

The devil (or whatever ruinous power that means) has adapted nicely to the New Age and it's harder to identify him. Since the arrival of DDT, one forgets about the Lord of the Flies. But there could be more than you imagine in a pack of Tarot Cards or a map of Atlantis. Then there was the craze about the Bermuda triangle. Now it is the daft shapes that have been "found" in fields of corn - and only ever in England.[9]

When I was young it was *"the most haunted house in Britain"*. Before that it was *"the Angel of Mons"*.

Aleister called them "a whisper of wonder that dazzles the brain - dreams born of the hope for a different reality!" He warned me about the New Age movement, and the Age of Aquarius.[10] He foresaw the pseudo cults and the coming glut of phoney gurus and teachers. "They will forecast the future by examining the lie of one's pubic hair," he said. "The occult will be sold as kits that one assembles oneself - the steeper the price, the closer you get to paradise."

I have nothing against New Age people as such, but are men free to believe what they want? No Master ever said that. Nobody has told us to elect God by democratic vote. Whether He, She or It exists or not is hardly a matter to be decided by the tabloid press. In the face of truth, opinion does not count.

Yes, you have free will to so choose between yielding and backing away, but you may change nothing. New Age people don't care about Masters. I have walked on air. I have walked on water. I have walked on the dark side of the moon. But they want to get their auras humming and make their alpha rhythms twang. Who cares how they perceive the gods? What's more important is, how the gods see them.

Aleister put it like this: "Lacking any compass, and having no guide, they will worship a mirror bought at a village fete." He shook his head in pity. "Sheep may safely graze, but men can think."

---

9. These were strange whorls and designs impressed in growing corn, but the hoaxers have now confessed.

10. I don't want to put astrologers out of business, but that is all that it is: a business. It is not done for charity. Michel Goquelin did not "prove" that astrology was an exact science as is often claimed. He said that there is a link between the season when people are born, the foods that are fed them, and their adult character. "Rain in May is worth a load of hay. But rain in July isn't worth a fly". My mother also says "A skinny winter makes poor babes". These are not trade secrets.

The Rest Home

It was a chilly morning. Lips were wreathed in mist. For some odd reason, a strange question was irking me and I couldn't get it out of my mind. "What do they do with bygone gods?" I asked. He stared out to sea like a portrait in oils. Perhaps he hadn't heard.

"At one time in history," I said, "this God is revered by the whole country. Yet the country is invaded and the people killed. What happens to the God?"

He regarded me oddly with his chin resting on his fist. Jutting upward, like the arrow that killed Cock Robin, was a cheap, wooden pen. Had I said too much or did he want me to go on speaking?

"Am I supposed to answer?" he barked. "If so, to what - the thought in your head or the noise that came out of your mouth?" His tongue could bite better than most people's false teeth and he was very sarcastic if anyone spoke 'murkily'.

My mind shot off like an edgy sheepdog, and rounded up my stray ideas. "If Gods stopped existing when we all forget about them, they would be no better than the fairies in 'Peter Pan'. They're not just ideas that we dreamed up ourselves, so they're not going to walk off-stage just because we boo them!" I gave a big shrug. "So where have they gone?"

"On a world cruise?" He blinked like a great frog. "Cookery class? Or perhaps they retired to an Old Gods' Home?" The fist beneath his chin became a finger on his nose. "What makes you think that they have gone?"

"Well nobody has seen them recently. The Red Sea hasn't opened very often lately. And if they are sending messages, then the post office does not deliver them."

"That was always the case! Even at their zenith, gods did not go shopping or open church bazaars. They did not stoop so low as to behave like members of left-wing parties the week before an election." He cleaned his nails with the pen-nib. "So as not to tamper with free-will, they must leave room for unbelief."

"But Gods wouldn't give a damn what people thought."

"I've just said that!" He smirked like a classics tutor who has just failed an athlete.

"Then where are they?

"Did you try at their last known address?"

My blood boiled. "I am being honest. You are being clever."

"You are being silly. I am showing you why." He paused. "You say they've vanished, on the grounds that you've not seen them. But when did you last look, and where? Why should they show themselves to you if to no one else."

"You know what I mean," I muttered.

"You are asking the wrong question of the wrong person," he snapped. "Ask them!"

"Ask who?"

"The Gods."

A dread drove round my mind like rain through a windy bus-shelter.

"The Gods have not gone," he said. "They have got new names."

8

SERKET

A scorpion goddess who causes the throat to breathe

No laughing matter

Since his own mother had been a she-wolf who ruled with a rod of iron, Crowley divined what feminism would be like. He was drafting 'The Book of the Law' while Queen Victoria was on the throne[1], while women marched for the vote, and while he was trying to audition scarlet women! We can say with some confidence that he was not a shearling lamb! He also knew just how unlovely women can be when you dispute their views.

"You can degrade her as much as you want," he said, "provided you say that you love her. In my career, the expression 'glorious bitch' has always been quite handy. If she is unbending, digs in her heels, I have found that 'mesopotamian strumpet' does the trick!" This, of course, was just a nippy way of calling her The Whore of Babylon. He was being naughty and winked broadly as he gave me this advice. "I'm sure that men father only angels, whereas women are born of donkeys. Try it, my boy! Feel free to have a go. If nothing else, you will see with your own eyes just how quickly a dainty lady changes into a *Tasmanian she-devil* !"[2]

It was hard to know what my father really thought about women. I don't think he hated them. On the other hand though, he wasn't obsessed with them either. "It's not that they hold any great glamour for us," he explained. "It is we who have a hunger. Love does not enter into it. Like the dog whose mouth waters when you go to the cupboard, we whine for the sweeties in her bottom drawers!"

On this topic he was very rarely elegant! In any case, his opinions changed from month to month, and the women he knew

---

1. This explains why it was so easy to produce in order to conceal The Book of Desolation.
2. Savage-looking, carnivore native to Tasmania, and reputed to be "unstoppable" if roused.

54

had a telling leverage on him. "Why can't they just be friends?" he once murmured, and I caught a glimpse of the man at the heart of the matter. It was almost an echo of Professor Dolittle, "Why can't a woman be more like a man?" The Women's Libbers should count him a hero since he never lied or tried to deceive them. He treated them the same, like items of luggage, and although there wasn't exactly a queue, there was no dearth of hopeful aspirants either. It has to be said that when Crowley devised the role of 'The Whore of Babylon' he plainly touched a nerve.

At the same time, he did show genuine concern for the spiritual progress of his ranks of lady friends. It was while I knew him, about 1943, that he was writing the famous letters to 'Cara Soror', which were published after his death under the title: 'Magick Without Tears', 1954. These were personal and honest. I don't believe that he had an eye on their future publication. As for my own mother, her private dream of being a film-star became true in the very way that he seduced her. That one night with him lit a flame that could never be quenched. But I cannot say that he loved her. He chose her. He revered her. She was the holy vessel.

"Never laugh at a woman," he told me. "She has no sense of humour as regards her own person. One misplaced joke, laddie, and she will shred your carpets, root out your piping, and transfix your scrotum with hat-pins." He timed his pause with all the skill of Sir Laurence Olivier. "A lady is no gentleman!"

It has been suggested that this kind of speech indicates a sort of castration complex on his part. Well, at the time in question, I wasn't trained so I could not very well explore the matter. But given that his mother had a vicious and prudish attitude toward sex, this is not out of the question. Then again, the very things that seem to have been a handicap, did in fact help him to make esoteric headway. He fathomed better than anyone else the magical nature of sexuality and its potential to hurt or to heal. When he chose, he could also be highly objective.

If he was right, then Women's Libbers will probably gnash every copy of my book to shreds. Which says something for their jaw muscles at least. Not many boors can do that![3]

"I do not much mind that women in politics are so very seldom

---

3. Boors or Boers = unchivalrous men. Boars = wild chauvinist pigs. (Sorry. It's in my blood.)

pleasant," said Aleister. "Being shouted at is better than being left on the shelf!" He had no reason to be vicious and these remarks were just his way of attuning his mind to the enigma of the modern woman. " After all," he continued, "if they are doubtful of their chances of landing a husband, then they have merely to abolish marriage and the whole problem is solved!".

He was being ironic. He knew as well as I do that men and women both need the kind of emotional security which is lost when we redesign the family unit.

"It is difficult to see," he said at another time, "that women were designed to run the world, any more than men were designed to be mothers." He still bore something of a grudge against "that Blavatsky woman". Nevertheless, he really did hold the view that in terms of magic, male and female had equal status. I don't think he was "a male chauvinist pig", as the poetess would say. I think he just disliked most women's character. It's a matter of taste and there's no point taking it any further.

"Far too many women believe that they ought to be liked," he observed. "But they make no effort to display the qualities that would make them likable. Make love to them, yes! For that they don't have to change anything. Nature gave them what they need, so it's nothing they should take credit for. What I object to is: all their cant and humbug." I need hardly add that Aleister could mock with burning contempt when he was that side out. "I smell a rat when they raise spurious details to make me miss the crucial points."

Even in his day, one or two voices proposed that God might be female. "What?" he would splutter with mirth. "They'll be saying next that He's a pansy! How do they know? How on earth do they know? It's what they'd like, so it's what they suggest; but where on earth are their reasons?"

If you managed to get him serious on such a silly subject he would ask them what the aim might be. "Is it perhaps to attract more church members and fill up the empty pews? Or do you intend to pander to women as if they were truly witches? Good heavens!" he cried. "We may not go around changing the sex of our Creator without so much as a by your leave! Mind you ..." he chuckled, "... it could explain all the scuffles in abbeys and nunneries."

Then, he came out with one of his deadly non sequiturs.

56

"Beside, I can't see Babylon letting a chance like that slip through its fingers. There would have been some comment, some mention. After all, you know what they're like, even today! Quite amazing the things that they can do with a camel!"

In a way, it does all seem so pathetic. After all, the hand that rocks the cradle is the hand that rules the world![4] If women don't like what men have done, they should blame their mothers. It is women who choose our toys when we are babes. And it is women who chip and chisel children into boys and girls before they reach school.

The Sex War
Be honest, ladies: you are losing the fight. I'd like to help but, well, a female fool is no better than a male one. How many of you fell into the trap I laid? It is an old ploy. You simply taunt the enemy until he (or she) flies into a rage. They then rush forward, blind and berserk. The results are very helpful:-
- *they forget any plan they might have had.*
- *they lash out wildly and fight in disarray.*
- *they tend to come at you solo, not as a platoon.*
- *they retreat in fatigue with their spirits dashed.*

The savage tribes of New Guinea do it. So do the gangs of teenagers in New York. If I may say so, without touching a sore point in France, it is how the Romans conquered the Gauls. The lesson you should draw is this: Keep Your Cool. Given that women have a natural tendency to be emotional, please heed my advice. With the greatest respect, ladies, never let men draw you into a slanging match. It's not your fault but ...
- *your voices are high and get strident with emotion.*
- *your frame is too dainty to match his exalted gesture.*
- *your lungs are too small to rouse the army at Agincourt.*
- *your rhetoric cannot beat theirs - they've practiced.*

Conclusion: choose some other terrain on which to fight, and select more telling weapons!

"Words alone," said Aleister, "will rarely win in court. One uses wit, scorn, dubious logic or anything at all that will impress the jury. They are only human beings when all is said and done. Beside that, the judge is probably a Mason!"

Feminism is doomed if you denounce men as monsters when

4.   W.R.Wallace, d.1881. Cited in 'Cyclopedia of Practical Quotations', J.K.Hoyt, 1896.

it's obvious that they're not. You have been too extreme and you have no more shot in your lockers. You were bitchy when you should have been subtle. You used too many foul words in your handouts, and you spoke in capital letters all the time. While you were chanting your chorus of slogans, likely converts slid softly out of the hall. You are boring. Your show is a flop. This is not the way to change the world.

Another thing you do wrong is the way you react to set-backs. You win a few, you lose a few, but you must not show your chagrin by behaving 'like women'! If you spit and scratch like alley cats, you only confirm the popular prejudice. *If you don't agree with your standard image, stop living up to it!* Don't shout. Do not scratch. Never display your fury. Purr like a panther as you lash him with his own smiling logic. Give him reason till he chokes on it.

If you are hurt, you'll want to hurt me back. Like son, like father, you'll say. Good. Like my father and like all the other masters, my aim is to balance the male and female aspects of nature and establish creative peace. If that's too flowery or nebulous, I can say it in plainer words. You should not be fighting to beat men, but fighting *to win them over*. They are not so much your enemy as your future allies!

I give the same message to my students, so you may trust me. I truly believe that men and women are equal. I shall not give you a lowly role and then up-grade the Virgin Mary just for your comfort. Nor will I juice you up with false promises of a superior status. The following seven rebukes are meant to help you:-
- *You did not discern your true power.*
- *The power you chose has been mis-used.*
- *You have plunged at the wrong target.*
- *The real target is alive and prospers.*
- *You have chosen bad arms and bad tactics.*
- *There is growing unease among your own members.*
- *The Lesbian cell is usurping the lead.*

"If females could plan as well as they scheme," Aleister said, "then they'd be up the mountain before us!" It was both a tease and a taste of truth. The mountain of which he spoke was *The Sacred Mountain*, which is both spiritual goal and the source of power.

58

Femmes Fatales

Dear old Aleister Crowley was all too well aware that men cannot resist a bit of sexual allure. "Where would the world be today," he demanded, "if Dil, Cleo, Sal, Big Kate, or Norma[5] had been less gorgeous?" In their own way, they were all feminists too - but instead of being over-awed by sex, they used it as an instrument of power.

Now magic is not going to help you retrieve your rightful status if you nurse any morbid symptoms or attitudes which go against nature. If tyranny is wrong in men, then it's also wrong in women! Forget about revenge and getting even, or you may put your mental balance at risk. Your only aim must be - to put the world to rights. Ladies! Women! Girls! Or whatever else you wish to be called. What great risks you are taking. You are ready to upset nature to support your theories when they are actually built on sexual stress.

You must have a few mental nurses on your list of members? Ask them about their patients. How many women seem to have been led to ruin or crushed by their own sexuality? It's also true of men's sacred virility, but many of them were mothered or married by what Crowley called "Black Widow Spiders". By that he meant viragos or Amazons who can only despise men and who secretly mock their sexual nature.

I am a Magician and so was my father before me. We both preferred to view things from a spiritual point of view, when and if possible. Being an occultist, he taught me that evil does exist. This is why I believe in entities (in human form or otherwise) who are driven only by negative forces.

The church invented the devil qua the contender for God's office and status, so let us continue using that term since it is so familiar. That devil, that rival for the throne of divinity, is clearly superior to we men. But he too, in his pride, has rebelled against the scheme of things and defied nature - so doesn't he just love any split between the sexes! In the midst of domestic quarrels, I can almost hear him smacking his lips with glee.

Just to shepherd us closer to an emotional suicide pact, he does what he can to stir up more trouble in the home - as if there wasn't enough already! What a way to destroy humanity: by

5. Delilah, Cleopatra, Salome, Catherine the Great, and (eerily prescient) Marilyn Monroe respectively.

laying traps and mines along the route of its creation! Whether you are male or female, you've got to admire his cunning!

I have noticed that the only way you can talk to a feminist is to say you totally agree with her. Like the cultural revolution in China many years ago, it's the only way to stop her waving that dratted little red-book in your face. But there will be no sober discussion. It will be as futile as telling Spain to close the corridas. She will see you either as a potential convert or a possible enemy. Show the least chivalry and you are branded for ever. If you begin by agreeing, the woman you are talking to no longer listens to you.

From the stance of an occult Master, she has a great deal in her favour. She has no need to invent she-gods, play at witches, or rewrite the books of ancient history to do it. It goes without saying of course, that there is not the least value in trying to use writers of fiction[6] as witness. I hesitate to dash your hopes but I have got to speak the truth. That truth states that feminism has no place in nature and that *it is properly to do with politics*. Since politics, as such, has no direct interest for me, I am not all that taken by feminism either. Except that it has now become so frenzied, it is a grave danger to personal health and the plans of the Gods.

Time, I think, for a nice cup of tea while you chew over those few morsels of advice. If you prefer to spit them out, you'll be given a bucket just before Armageddon begins.

---

6. Marion Z Bradley, author of 'Mists of Avalon' etc in which she re-works the Arthurian legends to support feminist views. Judging by the outcome for Britain, she over-estimates the value of "the goddess". If she is totally wrong, there is no reason why one should quote her.

9

SATET

The god of chaos who commands reverence and hostility

No Orchids for Miss Blandish[1]
I have to say that women do their case no great good at all by
claiming to be superior to men. The two sexes are as necessary to
each other as the front and back wheels of a bicycle ... unless, of
course, it is your ambition to be a clown! In this respect one can
only comment: how great has been man's anguish at coping with
his handlebar! A long time ago, a certain ancient tribe got
alarmed about the power that males and females exerted over
each other. In an attempt to rectify the problem they let all the
tyres down!

That tribe has been extinct[2] for a long time but the story
makes us go weak at the knees.

The male just shuffles the genes and helps nature to achieve
the next step. The goal is not a race of virgins who grow babies in
pods! That would be a step back in the direction of the ant-hill,
millions of clones from one breeding queen! Sex is neither a form
of female slavery[3] nor just a means of making babies. I'll go even
further: *the joy of orgasm is not important to physical health and life
would continue without it.*

Women have a natural role which embraces all that she is: her
body, her emotions, her relations, her work and even her ultimate
place in the scheme of things. There is nothing here which can
forbid or exclude a ritual role or someone who has dealings with
the beyond. They must accept this reality, and they must make

1. A celebrated gangster book, later a film, in which the 'Miss Blandish' of the title is a typical
   victim. Rather risqué at the time for its eroticism.
2. "Let the woman learn in silence with all subjection. But I suffer not a woman to teach, nor to
   usurp authority over the man, but to be in silence." (1 Timothy, 2:11)
3. It is one of the by-products of a sick society that men, much more than women, suffer sexual
   problems and resultant mental sickness, along with violence and a wish to kill.

men aware of it too. It is too wasteful to go out and win so why not simply become.

Men are not favoured if they are chosen to sacrifice themselves to the gods. Their progeny does not die with them for there are no unborn children lost and the tribe is unharmed. Men are not just seized by lust but by a powerful cosmic force which is seeking to be expressed. The sex event is thus able to be either positive or negative - a divine act or a diabolic one.

Docile husbands who stay at home and look after a baby? Yes, fine, until disaster strikes, until war breaks out, until the Gods call you to account.

It is said that women being more gentle than men, they would be less likely to go to war. What about Elizabeth I and Spain, or Mrs Thatcher and the Falklands? Who among the following world leaders was a pacifist: Mrs Ghandi, Mrs Bhutto, Mrs Mao Tse Tung, Mrs Cory Aquino, Ms Joan of Arc or even Queen Boudicca? Sorry ladies, but both history and medicine are against you, just as you will be against me simply for not agreeing with you. But before you have the vapours, scream, faint or stamp your feet, why not think about what I do say? It takes two to tango.

May healing balance all hormonal upsets, but the thought of two women in love is more piteous than that of two men, if only because of the un-lived babies. They have my sympathy but that can't make them happy. No, I don't just condemn feminism as an attempt to excuse the sexual deviance of a few. The link has been noticed though, and you'd all be wise to recognize it. No one is born gay. *There are no gay babies!* The matters arise much later out of events in early years.

If I am to go by what is written in the letters I receive, witches too are a species of Women's Libbers. It seems they have been chanting at me ever since my first book appeared. And I have been busy too, sending them all back. Has anyone developed a warty skin or got a broomstick stuck? I wonder of what creed it can be, and what kind of people could believe it, when the Goddess they worship is somehow offended by truth? Or is that just how certain key figures interpret the messages that are coming through?

I'm not comparing them to the priests of Baal. I do not liken myself to the prophet Elijah. But someone must pick up the gauntlet and teach them what is meant by the term "*righteous wrath*". Not mine! No, no, no, not mine. I'm speaking about the One you call "*your*" Goddess. I'm talking about the way some of you purport to "*know*" her wishes. If you're her servants and she's your Lady, I think you may have overshot the mark. I have mocked you but I have not mocked her. Do you have any right to believe she will mend your pride? Do you truly imagine I am a stranger to her?

Ill-met by Moonlight[4]

I cannot say how many times I may have met the Devil. I did not always catch on, you see. To be precise, I did not always believe that he existed. For no reason in particular, apart from personal preference, I assumed that the word was just a way of embodying a vague, abstract principle. I took it as a figure of speech, like *metonymy* or *oxymoron*. I imagined it was a symbol or perhaps even a joke. But I soon found out my mistake. That is why I must amend the first sentence.

The first time I knowingly faced Lucifer was in St Patrick's Catholic church in Soho Square, London. This is situated at the corner of a little side street in the district called the West End. I am glad to say that we were not introduced.

In those days, Soho itself was notorious as the red-light district of London, and Aleister took me there just to explain about 'trollops'. In the North of England, we have a speciality that we call 'collops'. These are thick slices of potato, dipped in batter, and fried. I therefore assumed that the trollops of Soho were some sort of variation on this tasty type of food.

I remember still how much this amused my father. But when he had finished laughing, he tried to give me a more helpful angle on the facts. He rather liked my error though. Forever after he was always saying that he would like to see one "battered".

But the purpose of our visit was serious and he pointed out a small building at the corner of the street. It had the austere air of a convent or even that of a prison. An official notice said it was an institute for the rescue of fallen women. I said it was a bit small for a hospital. Aleister held on to the railings and roared with laughter until his face went red.

---

4. The greeting of the fairy king, Oberon, to his queen, Titania, in 'A Midsummer Night's Dream', by Shakespeare.

When we entered the church itself, I felt rather overawed by it all. It looked like a film by W.G.Griffith: the pagan temple from 'Intolerance'. I mean no insult to Roman Catholics at all. I am just speaking the thoughts of an eleven year old Yorkshire lad who knew nothing but the plain chapel or simple churches.

It struck me as very exotic and strange. The heavy smell of incense made me ill at ease. The tortured statues and bleeding faces that peeped out of the gloom took me all the way back to the Chamber of Horrors at Blackpool! This was ghastly. In comparison with the parish church at Mirfield, this place was so filthy. The walls were stained with smoke. The statues, the niches, the arches and the woodwork were thick with layers of dust. As for the windows, they were so encrusted with grime that more light came from the penny candles.

Doubtless, I was as biased as hell, but this place didn't seem 'English'. Where were the flowers? Where was all the gleaming brass, the walls of radiant glass and the beaming rays of hope? Admittedly, I didn't go to my own church very often but at least they preached salvation there! Here it smelled of sin and tears, and the ambience was thick with the fog of purgatory. How could one be bullied into being good, I asked myself. Why would God come here where everything portends man's total lack of worth? As for Blake's Lamb of God, and a new Jerusalem, this was more like an abattoir.

Aleister began to explain the meaning of the Mass, and since I knew Latin, the sacred drama and ritual were stirring. All of a sudden, he made the sort of noise one does when vomiting. He spread his left hand over his belly, wheeled round, and just tore back the curtain of a box where they confess their sins. There was a priest inside. He did not jump or show any sign of surprise. He just glared at us like a vulture with a mixture of hunger and hate.

"Open for custom?" asked Aleister. "Or are you just observing life's rich cavalcade go by?"

The priest didn't move for a few seconds. There was just the clacking of rosaries, the murmur of prayers, and the cloying smell of incense and candle smoke. Then he drew himself up and took charge. "How did you know?" he asked mildly.

"First of all, the flies," rapped Aleister. "Then, alas, the smell. Do forgive me, old chap, but you could do with a good wash. Finally, the name inscribed on the door above your head, is that of a revered old priest who died a fortnight ago. You knew the box would be left empty out of respect. Yet you have put the red light on." He gave a grin and a shrug. "For fools rush in where angels fear to tread!"[5]

The pure contempt in my father's voice more than matched the tenor of his words. The priest just looked at him coldly. It was like a film where the burglar in the guard's grip says "it's a fair cop, guv'ner!" Except that at that point there was a sizzling, crackling plop, like an electric balloon being burst, followed by the slightest wind of incensed air gusting in to fill a vacuum. The box was empty!

A workman marched out of the baptistry which was situated nearer the West door. He was wearing blue overalls and carried a small tool-kit. He strode from the building.

"He must have been cross," murmured my father. "Normally he likes to leave in a puff of smoke. Well, that sort of thing is all right in 'Faust', but not in church."

The Train to Margate

On another occasion we were on our way to visit some friends of Aleister who lived on the outskirts of Margate. It was rather tricky to get to because there was a very important RAF station called Manston nearby, and our documents were checked several times en route. At all the stations there were posters issued by the Ministry of Information whose aim was to cut down on travel.

Aleister found one pasted on the door of the toilets and he stopped to inspect it with great gravity. It was made of cheap paper and asked quite simply - "*Is your journey really necessary?*"

He read aloud, and then looked round at all the men in earshot. "How can one possibly tell?" he gasped in mock wonder. "One feels the urge in one's bowels but it is difficult to weigh the intensity. One can give a verdict after but not before. If we all hesitate and follow the ministry advice, it could be too damn late! What? Quick, quick, the lavatory door - too late, too late, it's on the floor! You do see what I mean?" He appealed to everyone else within earshot. "What is done cannot be undone, to quote dear Lady Macbeth!"

Being English, the other occupants were quite nervous at simply being inside a public toilet at all. There are certain things,

5. Pope, 'An Essay on Criticism' (1711) 1,625.

and this is one of them, that an average type of British man believes is best done alone. It unnerves him to be among others, all standing in a row like lead soldiers. This timidity can be so grave that several men will leave the premises without, so to speak, having uncorked the bottle.

Here and now, with Aleister Crowley in fine voice, every single one of them was stricken stone deaf. With the expertise of practiced mimes, they shook the proverbial dust from their feet, and cleared off quickly in dribs and drabs. Since I could have put it more bluntly, I trust you'll pardon the expression. At the beginning I used to find it quite painful to travel anywhere with my father. He had no time to be tactful, you see. There were many times I wished he would be more discreet.

The railways were still in private hands in those days, of course, and different companies ran the networks in different parts of the country. Each had its own livery and all the carriages were painted in appropriate colours and bore a coat of arms.

The carriages then were still divided into three classes and naturally, my father and I always took the First. I say naturally but not because Crowley was in any way a snob. He was scathing about the quality of service and said very loudly that the inside of the carriages were "hosed down" from time to time. Even so, one stood little chance of keeping one's clothes clean! This annoyed him a great deal because he did dress quite superbly whenever he could.

This is also why he was able to adopt titles and pose quite happily as exiled royalty. He did this with the same sort of unconcern throughout his life. Actually he rather liked it and thought these new forms of address were much more fitting if he selected them himself! It was fairly obvious to me that he enjoyed living up to the fictitious role he created. He enjoyed taking people in. It was a kind of joke as far as he was concerned.

He made me join the game too. He told people that I was the boy-King Peter of Yugoslavia! It got me a free lemonade and an attack of the giggles.

Like any other specimen of healthy childhood, I made a bee-line for the seat that was next to the window. The glass was latticed with bands of sticky tape that was supposed to stop sharp splinters in an air-raid. There was nothing very much to look at. The names at all the stations had been effaced to make it more difficult for spies. I wouldn't have minded a spy, I thought, but I settled down to read a copy of 'The Beano'.

Just as I was getting absorbed though, I sensed the hair prickling on the back of my neck. I had already learned to trust this sign and I raised my eyes to look at Aleister. He was sucking in his cheeks and pursing his lips at the same time. This usually meant that he was taking aim. I followed the line of his eyes and saw the man in the corner by the door.

He was the only other person in the carriage and Aleister was staring at him fixedly with his face screwed up. The man's head was buried deep into a newspaper as if he were studying some race results or the closing figures from the Stock Exchange.

"Why does it cost more money in a first-class carriage," I asked trying to distract him. "I can't see that it is any cleaner than the others."

"If one wants the comfort, then one must pay the price," he replied. "For my own part, I don't mind the extra if one avoids dreadful company. Which is why I am puzzled," he boomed, "by that pathetic wretch over there."

This was enough to make my face go beetroot red. But when Crowley reached over and rapped on the stranger's newspaper with his stick, I tried to shrink into the moquette. "You there," he snapped. "You seem to have mistaken this room for the lavatory!"

As promptly as in any thriller film, the train plunged into a short tunnel. When we emerged into bright sunlight just a few seconds later, the corner seat was empty. I swear the door had not opened. There had been no noise nor any draught. But there in the cushion where he had sat, a hollow was still slowly filling.

"At least he's taken the hint," said Crowley.

"You call that a hint?" I asked, and my father just shrugged. "What made you think that anything was wrong?" I went on. "He didn't do or say a thing."

"The silly fool was reading a newspaper, for god's sake!"

"Lots of people do that."

"Not one that is nearly thirty years old."

"You couldn't see the date. You hadn't got your glasses on."

"I could see the headline," he said in a ratty voice. "Look for yourself!"

He tossed it to me. I was still no wiser. "It's just about the war," I said.

67

"Exactly," he snapped. "But The Great War, not this one."

The majority of people are under sixty years old. So they may not realize that the Great War was the one between 1914 and 1918. It was renamed The First World War after The Second World War had finished. Even then, the people who had lived through it kept on using the more familiar term.

When I bent to look at the date on the newspaper I saw that it was 1914. I was quite stunned. Not by the events that had just happened but by the fact that the paper seemed so fresh. My mother lined the drawers each spring and in only twelve months, newsprint usually turned yellow. This was as white as the day it was first printed.

"Smell it," he ordered.

"What?"

"Stick your nose in the middle and take a sniff."

I did. "Roast chestnuts," I told him.

"There you are, you see? Just as I thought."

Even to this very day, I have not been able to work out what he meant by that remark.

10

MESKHENET

The goddess who presides at childbirth

An Encounter in Paris

Quite obviously, there is no way that I can be certain who, or what, these persons were.

I can't even swear that it was the same one on each occasion, although I feel pretty sure about it. I was surprised that my father did not seem the least bit fearful.

Far from it, to tell the truth. He looked and sounded as if he were indignant, like an old colonel with a gouty foot. Naturally I asked him about it. I mean, one cannot be neutral or pretend to ignore it when the person you are with starts lashing at the public with a very stout cane!

He didn't explain though, or not in so many words.

"It is every person's duty to learn how to recognize his own evil," he said. "Every one of us is supposed to calculate how best to confront it for himself. It is one of the biggest steps that novices can take."

He looked at me a little sadly and then shrugged. "It's no good counting on me, you know. I cannot protect you for ever because, to put it simply, I won't always be here. You have to learn how to cope for yourself. Part of my job is to teach you how to manage." He shook his head as if the truth were somehow difficult to face.

"It's a bit like learning how to drive a car, my lad: you will have to understand all about signs, signals and gestures that policemen make. How shall you protect others if you can't even take care of yourself?" He ruffled my hair and took hold of my chin. "Be a magician, my son. Go forth and fight your dragons! I will keep my fingers crossed and wish you good luck!"

As it happens, I haven't done too badly, I think. I followed his advice and on the whole I seem to be winning. Mind you, I've met that person again. There was a time in Paris that I remember very well. Oh, it's something like seven years ago, and I stayed at a moderate hotel in the Marais. On my first morning, I strolled along to the new shopping centre which was not yet quite finished, built on the site of 'Les Halles'. This had been the Parisian version of the old Covent Garden - the wholesale food market.

I was going down the moving stairs when a young man snatched my sacoche. This is the male equivalent of a handbag and is extremely common on the continent. In England, as you might expect, it is looked on as very 'feminine'. There was everything in it - English money, French money, passport, credit cards - the lot!

I stared hard at his receding back and, when he stepped off at the bottom, he turned to look back at me. He froze. As I caught up with him, he simply handed me the bag. A young gendarme was watching with a funny look in his eye. I said nothing. I just took the bag and remounted the escalator to go back to street level.

I was puzzled. Why pick me? What made me a likely victim? And why did he wait to give back my sacoche? I am not a practical man and I would have been crippled by the loss of documents. So I was just horrified at the prospect. I did not mutter a spell. I made no magical sign. I was too damn shocked to think. So all I could do was stare at him.

The gendarme had followed. There was a small police station almost facing us.

"Excuse me, sir. That young man, what had he been up to?"

"My bag slipped off my shoulder," I said. "It fell down a few steps."

"I know him, sir. He is very well known to all of us. You are sure he did not rob you?"

"But he did not try to keep it," I replied. "He gave it back to me. You saw him yourself."

"Excuse me for having disturbed you, sir. But that was a fucking miracle."

This all passed in French, though the gendarme recognized my accent. If he reads this book, perhaps he would care to contact me and confirm my story.

St Eustache

It took me a while to get back to normal. I just wandered along the streets around Les Halles, not paying very much attention to where I was going. Somehow or other, I found myself outside a very large church named after Saint Eustache. It didn't mean anything to me. I supposed it must have been the equivalent of the English name, Eustace. But then, I had no idea who he was either. St Bede and St Alban, that's about my limit.

I went inside. I suppose I meant to sit down and take the weight off my feet for a few minutes. I wandered about like a restless dog when suddenly my eye was caught by a vivid piece of modern art that looked so off-key in a church. It was a lively model of a typical market. It was done in low relief, and a small notice explained that the artist wished to celebrate the ancient link between this house of God and the vicinity.

I don't remember the piece in any great detail. There were all kinds of food in baskets and crates. There were stalls and wagons and people. Taken as a whole, it was an eloquent image of the noise and flurry of a busy market. It was one of those rare works of art into which one can project oneself and become lost, so to speak.

Suddenly, one of the solid figures in the sculpture turned its head and smiled at me!

I was not mistaken. I blinked. I looked at the roof for a moment. He was still smiling when I dropped my eyes again. This time he lifted one of those belts with pouches on them - the kind of thing that traders wear round their waist. Now it was my holdall and he waved it at me.

I turned my head away and stared straight before me toward the altar. Some fifty yards ahead a sitting figure turned its head - and it was identical to the miniature in the sculpture.

I felt the hairs on the back of my hand tickle as goose bumps rose on my arms. The person in front stood up and walked up the main aisle as if to reach the door. He stopped just at my side and looked past me at the sculpture in the chapel.

"How very singular," he said.

"And that much more valuable for not being legion," I replied. I was making what I thought was a subtle allusion to the scriptures. In the Gospel of St Mark (5,ix), the Devil is quoted as having said "My name is Legion: for we are many". I think he

71

was jeering at the One-ness of God and trying to boast of his own prestige. That is why he used the royal "we".

Evidently my devil was not impressed. "I never said that," he snarled. "They put the words into my mouth."

I was in no mood to discuss such abstract details. "Do you see the newspaper on the floor by that stall?" I said, pointing my finger. His eyes turned to the colourful piece of sculpture. "It's yours, I think, and you have not finished reading it."

He moved swiftly to the sculpture and started shrinking. His eyes were full of hate as he stepped back and joined the frozen crowd.

"How did you know?" I heard him whisper.

"You stand out like a sore thumb," I murmured, "or a red warning light."

If that statue is still in the church of St Eustache, then so is that particular devil - waiting perhaps for someone else to wink at.

Against Nature

My father gave scant thought to sexual deviance and never wrote about it. He did have an opinion though, and I have already alluded to it. Here it is in a nutshell: nobody is born gay - they become gay later! Today, more and more doctors are coming round to share this view. It isn't very popular among the gay culture though since it pulls down one or two of their own pet beliefs.

Needless to say, he did not consult Mme Edith Cresson. She would have been much too young in those days. She had yet to make her name as the French Prime Minister who dropped more bricks in two weeks than others do in two years. One of her pearls of wisdom really would have stunned him. She said that one quarter of all English males were gay. "How does she keep count?" he would have asked. "Oh yes, yes, I see now. Well, the poor, dear lady must simply get used to *La Politesse Anglaise*. In other words, pretending to be gay *is a man's way of ignoring a woman's wink!*"

He knew what he was talking about, of course. He'd had wives and women galore and dallied with not a few men. "It's very much overrated," he once said. "Making love to a man is a bit like playing football with your socks on your head."

Neither he nor I have been hostile, yet gays are likely to be

72

annoyed with me. It helps them cope with their guilt problems to believe they were born that way. It makes them feel less culpable and lends a sense of false security. But when I say otherwise, it's not because I want to smack them in the teeth with a rotting fish. Far from bearing them any ill-will, I believe that they can be cured.

Even as I say it, I can hear their howls of fury. They may not want a cure. They deny that they need a cure. In their own opinion, and they claim to be experts, they are not tainted with any illness so they do not require therapy. They have my sympathy and my best wishes.

Just to make it quite clear though, neither I nor Aleister Crowley has ever called it a disease. But we have always said that being gay is an abnormal outlook on life. I have heard all those tedious myths about it nursing genius, about it causing the culture of ancient Greece, and about all of us being gay at heart.

The divine Sarah Bernhardt was once asked for advice by a very young, would-be actress. "Go forth and suffer," she is reputed to have replied. But there is no evidence at all to support this idea or to show that actors "suffer" any more than any other calling. They are more likely to talk about it, that is all!

It is all totally false, I'm afraid. The posture does give some comfort, but only for a very short while. It performs the same function as a baby's dummy, you see. It works fine as a stopgap, but it cannot replace the real thing.

The majority of talents and abilities are innate, and only a few are added during infancy. A genius is no more and no less likely to be homosexual than any other person. About one in ten men are gay and, if anything, genius is slightly less frequent among them than among straight men. All that this fact proves is that there is no connexion between the two factors.

But it is a fact that inverts are more obvious, so when one of them achieves a certain fame, his sexual tendency is noticed. It is silly to divide the world up into 'geniuses' and 'gay geniuses'; that is as much a political gesture as saying their are 'oranges' and there are 'South African oranges'. As we all know, oranges occur in the best regulated families.

Yes, it is true, that one in umpteen thousand babies is born fully equipped with a set of both male and female sex organs.[1]

---

1. They are called androgynes or hermaphrodites.

This is the only true inter-sex and luckily they happen to be very rare. Absurdly, and for causes too complex to go into, such a baby may escape notice for several years.

I knew of one case which was noticed only when "he" was being shaved for abdominal surgery.

As soon as possible, one tries to change them into one sex or the other, according to their psychic make up. In virtually every case, they want to be the sex that they have been raised as. In other words, they stick to the one selected by their parents at birth. They find it easier and it takes the least amount of mental effort.

They do not try to argue with the facts. They make no effort to wriggle out of it. But please notice: the hormones in their blood do not determine even their conduct. The crucial factor is almost always the way they were brought up. This it is which decides how they think, feel and behave. They are truly free to choose whether to be male or female, and still their internal feelings are what they have been taught to be.

Innuendo

With gays though the matter is almost purely emotional, so they do argue and they do protest. They do not want to be stuck with the conduct that is "appropriate" to their genetic sex. They live in a state of constant red alert, one part of their psychic radar searching for sexual contacts and another part guarding against the chances of rejection and attack. Small wonder then that they get quite a kick out of causing shock and outrage to others. They are not just open, they flaunt themselves. Not only do they refuse to conform but also seek applause.

Since they can get all the rapture they want, and since their campaigns gain little extra support, one must ask why they behave that way. Either it gives a feeling of relief from any burden of guilt or it takes their minds off other anxieties. One thing is clear - they are not calm or cool or collected, and they show many symptoms of neurosis.

I'm sorry if this puts the cat among the pigeons. If I know them as well as I believe, they will now raise their eyebrows and mount an attack on me. "There is a reason," they will say with heavy innuendo, "why a so-called occult Master is so absorbed in

2. This is the gay term for a man who hides the fact of his homosexuality and tries to live a "straight" or normal life.

the subject."

Oh yes, my dears! What a typically childish way of reacting - to dodge the question by attacking the person who raised it! Well, sorry to disappoint you but, no, I am not a 'closet queen'[2] myself! But even if I were lying, which I'm not, how would that help your argument? Scratching your opponent's eyes out does nothing to suggest he's wrong. Attacking his character is just so much easier, I suppose. But then, being catty is part of the myth.

Why should my opinion upset them? What does it matter what I think? I'm not the Pope. I can't place them under interdict. I'm not a famous Law Maker who can define what they do as criminal. I am just a poor magician. But then, the world has attacked magic and occultism throughout the ages, which is why I can understand. So why does criticism infuriate them so much? Why do they get so much more excited than any other social group?

No, their desires do not repel me. I don't break out in cold sweat when I meet them. I am not trying to get a distorted revenge on my mother, my father, or a friend who dropped me. As a matter of fact, I do not wish them any harm at all. I simply want to help those among them who are still open to help. So do come on: don't be mean about it. It is not really in your interest to swell your numbers by enrolling the young and the lost. Admit it: you are so keen to convert that you may sometimes do harm without wishing it. Please - be fair.

I hope I have done something to clear the air and not make you my enemies. I don't like enemies of any type. We all have enough with the civil service being what it is. So why am I getting at you? Why do I have a bee in my bonnet as regards gay folk? Ah, well, you see, you must stop burbling about civil rights and howling your rancour at God, the Government and Guys who married. When you have quietened down, these facts remain:-

- *I am a genuine magician.*
- *I know how power can be turned to evil ends.*
- *There's a lot of power generated by sex.*
- *Unhappy people attract "bad vibes".*
- *Gays are prone to depression and suicide.*
- *I would like to stop that.*

Will that do for a start? I've been trying to get your attention, that's all.

11
SAH

The constellation of Orion, visible only at night

Bad Motives

Being gay is not natural. This makes it difficult (but not impossible) for a gay person's soul to flourish or achieve its destiny.

That's not exactly tactful if I want to sell more books. I know that I'd outstrip 'Scarlett' if I told you only what you wanted to hear.

That is why the Music Hall was so popular, and quite a few "artistes" use the same gimmick today. It's one of the oldest tricks in the trade: flatter your audience. Get them to sing. Let one of them come on stage and be sawn in half. Turn the show into a talent contest! It's so obvious, don't you see? Every salesman, every Don Juan, and every con-man uses it! Get the audience to applaud themselves and they tell the world how good you are. It happens every night of the week on television.

I do not mean to harm gay people at all. They can be charming folk and they deserve our respect. But that doesn't mean they are '*natural*'. It isn't natural to be born blind or a dwarf. Yes, it happens - but it shouldn't! Being gay is contrary to the plan. It is not what nature intended. It even works against her. Don't be angry with me for stating the truth. We have to be honest because - well - there are outcomes.

There are gay coppers, gay politicians, and even gay hussars. There are gay priests too to give you peace, and gay doctors to ease your stress. None of which makes deviance any more 'right' or 'proper'. You may think it is no one else's affair, but you are wrong. It is our society you are living in. If you try to change it without our approval, we may clamp down again. There are more of us than you.

76

I don't mean to sound hostile. I just want you to realize how society will react if you go on. You're not just looking for equality - *you are elbowing to the front.* The tolerance and the sympathy will not last for ever. You are testing the limits already, and when AIDS gets worse - all the old bigotries will come out of the closet. Now listen: it's no good asking people to be reasonable *when you've not been reasonable yourself!*

We are not all that worried about whom you love, or the way that you express your love. We are not children and *we do not doubt the depth of your emotional sincerity.* But your sexual antics might even be amusing, in the same way that throwing folk to the lions once was! In other words, my friends, you could become scapegoats and, God knows, you don't half stick your necks out. That is the nub of the problem.

You insist on being seen and, let's be honest, on trying to recruit new members. It's a bit like being a smoker, I suppose: you know you shouldn't but you like it. Hence there is guilt. Because there's guilt, there has to be defiance. And one finds courage by increasing one's numbers.

Voting Power

In a democracy, the rules and laws are determined by majority vote, but matters of morality are not. Human judges are not competent to deal with right and wrong. *Neither are gays.* The law deals with criminals but The Beyond deals with those who offend against Nature.

But I'm talking of something more than just right and wrong. True, a court did once accuse a cock of being a witch, and condemned it to death for refusing to confess! That was blind stupidity. But while black magic is rife in graveyards, parks and derelict flats, the police do nothing because no law is broken. It is not illegal to worship the devil.

The same is true of drug addicts or drinkers - they like to spread it around. They enjoy infecting others with the same deadly habits. So they too are unwelcome in society, and they too form a new culture with its own language, meeting places, and secret rules. It is all to do with solitude and isolation. But the losers go too far. They have no right to howl down the truth simply on the grounds that they don't like it. Saddam Hussein does that. Hitler did it too. It is typical of tyrants. It is also

77

typical of gays when one exposes the weakness in their arguments.

It is silly to use agitprop campaigns. They do nothing to prove a case one way or the other. It is easier to mock a person than his cause. It is easier to reason falsely than to answer truth. For example, one may list all the famous people who were homosexual, but what does it prove? How does that justify your stance? If we go back as far as the Emperor Hadrian, you'll find many of them had smallpox too. When a man defends himself before he has been accused, it makes the jury jumpy.

You are men and women who refuse to make babies. You are the ones who cannot build conjugal bliss. You will not grow old in the bosom of a growing family. You will never know the quiet joy of playing with your own child's children. Is it merely chance that you also have a higher suicide rate?

Now be fair. Is it wrong of us to worry about these things? Is it bad of us that we want to stop you preaching to our kids? You have no moral right to claim that your way of life is as good and natural as any other. It is not true. You are morally wrong if you try to convert others. Neither society, nor God, will stand idly by and permit that to happen.

You may believe your own words but I doubt it. You snatch at false facts to try and justify your stance and improve your status. But you can't change the truth to make it more suitable. You may not distort reality to plead your special cause. If you lie to yourself, you may unhinge your brain.

How absurd, for example, that gays should ask to adopt babies. Yes, it is a natural urge to wish to be a parent. It is normal to become one if it is done by natural and not artificial means. When you wilfully choose *not to sow your seed*, you are in no position to demand your share of the harvest. Neither may you seek amends for damage you have done to yourself over the years.

The Reason Behind All Things
How could you *not* pass on your own values to the young in your charge? Oh don't cite films like '*La Cage aux Folles*'. The author was an actor, that's all. He had no special training as an expert on the subject. Besides which, it was a comedy that he wrote - something we were meant to laugh at in order to relieve our stress.

With all the sympathy in the world, society dare not let you convert its young. Be fair about it. At least choose targets which are old enough to know and strong enough to defend themselves. In this respect, I dare say the Parachute Regiment is fair game. Try your luck with them. From what I hear, many of them are no better than they should be.

If you claim equal rights, then you must accept equal responsibility. You must submit to the same rules that apply to heterosexual people. But that is not enough, it seems. You are getting furious. I quite agree that you should be accorded the widest possible freedom - that is conducive to peace and order. If you demand more, you are in the wrong. If you take more, then you should be punished. It means that you are deluded by the forces of chaos.

How weird that women's lib and gay lib have somehow come together in the last decade. They both use dubious argument e.g., "If I and my friends are like this, then it must be natural, and what God intended." They have fallen right out of a cartoon.

My father is not best remembered for his sexual reserve, and he did have congress with one or two men. This is enough for certain people to clap hands with glee and chant "Aleister Crowley was one of those!" I would have thought his numerous children would have scotched that rumour! At all events, even he said "No!"

Neither he nor I, nor any other magician, would ever deny the energy that may be generated by sexual acts between men. But when we use the term *man* or *male* we are not sticking with mere biology or anatomy. We are pointing to virility, and by that we mean the *father force* or the *male force*.

When I speak of gays, I am referring to people *who have made a choice*. They would claim the choice wasn't theirs. You are what you are because of the journey you took across the board. The many moves may have been either easy or hard, obvious or obscure, forced or relaxed. But you did have the choice and, as far as a magician is concerned, you are still free to make remedial moves.

In other words, the homosexual can come back to the main track instead of staying stuck up the dead-end where he was shunted. It is up to you, of course. You stay as you are or you change. Magic can help. If you are totally honest, what have you got to lose?

Straight people do not hold marches or mount a crusade for the simple reason that they are 'normal' and so they bear no stigma. They feel quite safe and are somewhat smug about it. If they are uneasy about their sexual identity then they may be bigoted too. I see symptoms among the fascist ranks: young men who are too tough and too macho. Some of them are less like gallant knights than cracked records.

They are not natural either. Like some gymnasia and clubs for the Martial Arts, there are lots of people trying to 'boost' their dose of masculinity and to conceal their real inclinations which terrify them. It is hard to say that they are 'happy'.

In any case, it is futile to claim that their instincts are different. Human beings do not have instincts any more. They were far too rigid to allow the species develop so they were ditched several millenia ago. Our large brains give us a clear advantage since we have an almost limitless capacity to learn. But we learn from both our parents - and to ensure that there are usually two, sexuality keeps male and female together.

Hormonal imbalances can exist. But if we use this fact to explain away homosexuality, we are as good as conceding that it is an illness.

Optimist or Outcast?

All conduct is taught and the patterns are given to us by the world in which we live. This means that 'normal' is what the community wants, and what most of its members accept. A minority view may be helped, but they must never claim greater respect than the larger group. Stark survival is the matter at stake. Sexual deviance does not improve its chances of being accepted merely by claiming it is popular. On the contrary, the more the gays protest, the greater the world's alarm. You simply may not argue that the majority is wrong.

On the whole, gay men are more *feminine than women*. They are giving a potted parody of all the queens in history. As for lesbian women, they can be more mannish than men. They look and sound like rugby forwards at a booze-up. I know I sound cruel. But how else can I get you to consider a serious proposition? All these people are putting stress on some signals and draping veils over others - and they do it in spite of nature!

In fact, they make a conscious choice to go against nature, and it is purely for *emotional* reasons. If it were normal then there'd be no need for such a desperate struggle, and there would be no call for all the rubbish that is spoken.

They out-herod Herod, as Shakespeare puts it.[1] They go too far and they are too defiant. In eighty per cent of cases, this improper sexual identity is a bit of despair and a bit to spit in the world's face. I must not neglect to mention that AC's reason for being the Great Beast was mainly to spite his mother! That is significant!

My own problem is: I don't really wish to hurt or offend any of you. I want to bring you to your senses. If you are like this or like that, I don't want you to waste your chances by binding yourself to it for ever. To claim equality *you must live life and not a fairy tale.* You must be full citizens. You do not score a point by profuse display - you are only mocking your own kind. Accept it or not but the facts are against you, and the vast majority of people are NOT like you. You are a minority and you are angry, and you are trying to make yourself heard.

But please, do not rise to the bait. Do not let them just shrug you off. You want, and you merit, freedom from bigotry and menace. You cannot have the same benefit unless you obey the same laws. You cannot both claim freedom and also offend the liberty of other people. Otherwise you fall into the trap that has been set for you, since freedom does not give you license to destroy.

The Lord of Misrule uses your anguish to turn you into an 'inner foe' of society. I would have said The Lord of the Flies. It is a much older title. But gays don't much care for having their leg pulled. Yes, you may love your own sex. It is not taboo, except to certain Police Chiefs who are sensitive on the point. There are people like you in every walk of life - military, politics, law and even religion. To be quite factual, some of our own occult members are like that too.

But the really strange thing about gays is the extent to which their gayness obsesses them. Doesn't that fact alone suggest that something is wrong? They don't just think about it - they live it. They set about it with all the zeal and verve of hit-men. Being gay is a full-time occupation.

1. Hamlet, the speech to the players, III.ii.

A Significant Difference

Gay men go looking for more sexual partners per week, than ordinary men have in a year! That is one hell of a big difference. Also they seek more orgasms per month than most of us could tolerate. That is another big difference.

Do they need all this just for sexual relief? If the answer is yes, then in what sense do they need it - because this too is an important difference. Are they using quantity to make up for the lack of quality? Or are they trying to compensate for some other missing factor - one to be found only in straight sex? Before they deafen us with their howls of denial, just remember that *they have no way of knowing*! What they say on this topic is neither qualified nor unbiased. Gays are not neutral witnesses.

Is there any value at all in asking drug addicts whether we should legalise cocaine? They will say it is terrific, of course. They don't give a damn about long-term mortality. But whether they approve or not, pleasure is not a valid test except in the world of Nintendo! In any case, the delight that deviants derive from their forays does not even satisfy their own bodily needs. Oh yes, in a certain emotive aspect, it means a lot to cuddle and love someone of their own sex. But that too is a habit that can be acquired. Ask a sailor.[2] Ask a man who has been in prison for a long time. They confess that it goes on. But it is for lack of anything better and nothing to do with how they are made!

If you ask murderers, they are not on the whole in favour of the death penalty. No prisoner believes he had a fair trial. All hunters believe that foxes are vermin. All immigrants say we have no right to turn them back. Muslims think that any country they live in would be better off if the Mullahs ran it. Manufacturers of mineral water think that wine causes heart disease, and cigarette sellers can prove there is no link between smoking and lung cancer!

Gays say God is wrong. Women's Libbers say Nature made a mistake. They deny the facts as the world perceives them. So we are wrong and they are right. Would everyone please change his opinions! I advise them to be careful. They are on the brink of grave sacrilege. When all of creation is meant to march in step, and all things have been made to harmonize, then woe betide the

---

2. Even Winston Churchill referred to the navy as "...rum, sodomy and the lash." Sir Peter Gretton, 'Former Naval Person', Chap 1.

pride that defies the Infinite! Stop worrying about what you want. Pause a moment and ask what the Gods want. Or have they too been swept aside as obstacles in your path?

Perhaps sex serves many different needs and not just the one we are most familiar with. I would not dream of handing down any kind of verdict. I don't give a damn about their stopgap for jollity except that it blocks the route toward true success. I am totally neutral about who makes love to whom - so long as there is no force nor any risk of iniquity.

As for sex with children, it is heinous. Child abusers find comfort from numbers, no doubt, so they form cliques and print leaflets, but they are evil men. Strength of appetite is no excuse, for if you can't control it, you are mad. You cannot allay regrets with lies. You just degrade your species, insult nature and spit in the face of the gods. A thousand ghosts will gather in the dark and the night air will wriggle with demons as thick as lice. Seek treatment now before your mind is lost or shredded and you die on a dirty mattress in a lunatic asylum.

All that said, I must quote my father again. "The most hermetic[3] of all magical powers can be raised and summoned by men loving men." He would then smile, amused by people's reactions.

"It reminds me of the time a bishop was visiting a school. 'What is the Holy Trinity?' he asked one child who suffered from a cleft palate. 'Three persons in one god', came the nasal reply. 'I'm sorry, said the bishop, but I don't understand.' The child sniffed in a superior way. 'You're not supposed to understand, said the child. It's a Mystery'!"

3. To begin to tackle this enigma one must really understand what the term 'hermetic' means. The problem for many occultists is that they presume to know already.

12

HENET

A pelican goddess who aids spirits through the underworld

Bumps in the Night

How can we believe that a spirit realm exists? Many sincere people are already convinced but that doesn't help the others: the ones with serious doubts to overcome. Queen Victoria was quite obsessed by the subject, which explains why, after her death, Princess Beatrix tore out many of the pages from her mother's diaries. Most likely they talked of spirit seances and miracles which the Queen, a gullible widow, believed that she had seen.[1] It is said that her descendants are also deeply interested in the subject. But even the most massive royal support does not prove the reality of spirit beings.

By exactly the same token, if I had proof which nobody else accepted, I'd continue to believe, albeit as a minority of one. I would not be in the least bit worried that I was alone in my certitude. Christ was alone and, according to the Bible, He spoke both with God and with evil spirits. The one thing you should not do is treat the matter with lofty disdain.

This question about the spirit realm is just about the most critical thing anyone could think about. It doesn't matter how many sceptics there are. It doesn't matter what rank and status they hold. Witnesses are just as valuable whether they come from the slums or a stately home. All that said, people do tend to get very heated on the subject.

If you don't believe, you are quite hostile toward those who do, and vice versa. Why, should this be, I ask? What is the reason for this mutual antipathy? We wouldn't argue anywhere near as strongly about matters to do with diet - whether one should eat fish or meat. We wouldn't get worked up at all about the relative

1. cf. Peter Underwood, 'Queen Victoria's Other World', Harrap, 1986.

84

merits of Beethoven or Brahms. So why does this matter of spirits seem to throw the fat in the fire and cause such an outburst of emotion?

The answer is not far to seek. Just think what would happen if the existence of spirits was proved. Imagine what would follow as a logical consequence. We'd have to re-work all our ideas and attitudes. Many of our opinions would have to be changed. Why, it could affect our whole way of life. In some people's view, it is therefore much wiser not to look! The very idea engenders a kind of deep fear. I think it brings back ancient ideas that slumber still in the foundations of your soul.

"Don't tell me," you cry. "I don't want to know."

What? Are you still as juvenile as to imagine that if you stay deliberately ignorant then you can plead innocence? That is not so, I fear. Block your ears to the voice crying in the wilderness, and you condemn yourself.

But since many of us are cowards we do not go any further than that. We want to stay sceptic. We couldn't cope with the other thing. So we avoid finding out and we turn away from all offers of insight. It doesn't matter being wrong, we declare, if we don't realize we're wrong. What a clever thing to say! What a cunning way to put it. If I'm not right, don't breathe a word - isn't that entitled 'The Creed of the Hypocrite'?

Enticing the spirits to rap tables, or even turn them, is an easy way of finding out if they are present. If nothing happens you cannot be sure either way, but if there is a 'prodigy' then that is quite massive evidence in their favour. This is just how they felt in the late 19th century when dabbling with the spirits was as popular as a parlour game. In fact, interest was so enormous that a toy factory started making the Ouija Board as a mass product, and it is still available today. It is simply a small, flat board mounted on free castors which can move in any direction at the lightest touch. The name means "the yes-yes board".

At the time, a new religion[2] began, which accepted psychic events as proof of life after death. We must also observe that this was the era of 'Variety' or 'Music Hall' types of diversion. The 'Top of the Bill', or 'Star of the Evening', was often a legendary magician of the theatre, whose exciting effects have never been repeated since. As if this were not enough, throw in the dramatic

---

2. The National Spiritualist Church, with branches in several countries.

and awesome news of fabulous treasure being found in Egypt. Join it all together, stir the pot, and what you have now got brewing is: *an occult revival of the highest quality*.

It was an exciting period to be alive. For us, here and now, it is just impossible to realize how pivotal such things were, or how seriously people took them. This they certainly did but, rather oddly perhaps, they did not treat it with any great gravity. They were less dazzled by it than we are by new space projects, tearing energy from the Pacific Ocean, or creating food out of sewage! Their attitude was odd, to say the very least.

Yet the truth was that, for most of them, ghostly stuff like this had nothing to do with religion. It was just seen as jolly good fun and perhaps an erudite pastime. They approached it rather in the same frame of mind as curious infants who are excited to learn how the things work. But they had no sense of anything strange going on so they took it all quite quietly. Like 'Trivial Pursuits' or 'Mutant Turtles', it was nothing more than an amusing game or a craze that came and went.

You see, it did not occur to the churches to denounce it ... well, not with any great strength at any rate. I think that everyone of rank or standing knew that if they pointed out the possible dangers, this would only have made it much more tempting still. So no one tried to link it with worship of the devil or sorcery. It was simply not suggested.

If you had proposed it, they were so sloshed on Darwin remember, they would have howled you down with derision! How in God's name could such a thing even be naughty, let alone harmful? It was all part of the great 19th century march toward science, knowledge and a happier world. This much was sure: the application of science had nothing to fear from old wives' tales. Quite ironic really, when doctors died of cancer through messing with X-rays.

Exorcism Old
In the year 1900, my father Aleister Crowley was a smart young graduate of only twenty-five years. He had been born, and raised, during this fabulous era of iron, industry and steam. Despite the fact that his family frowned on all forms of 'dabbling', his own interest was very much captured - one might say, inspired. So there

we have it! Four of the themes, the strands that entwined like plaited tresses all through the rest of his life: Magic, Egypt, Sex and Spirits. It gives a whole new meaning to the snide phrase: Aleister Crowley's life was a total MESS.

In my own student days, there were lengthy queues to join The Occult Club. They were all terribly keen to learn about ESP[3] and apply it, if possible, during exams. There were also a number who rather fancied having a go at a spirit seance, for similar reasons. Those who found it all too humdrum, opted instead for the panting pleasure of a great and fearsome rival, the Ghost Club. They held meetings at midnight when they pricked a pin into a list of haunted houses and all trooped off to lay the phantoms - or sometimes their wenches. There was a striking increase in sore throats but one couldn't tell if it was due to howling or loafing on wet grass.

In those days, of course, films like 'Freddy' had not yet been conceived. If they had been, they would scarcely have put us off. It was the cheapest pastime within reach - apart from sex of course. Even there it won hands down. One, the passion was so great that our spirit stayed hot. Two, the coldest nights provided even better thrills, what with clinging mists, snapping twigs and the crunch, crunch of feet in crispy grass. Three, the result was much improved by a bottle or two of beer. It gave one heart. It braced one's backbone. Or as we say in the North, it woke the sodding ferret up.

Things did sometimes get out of hand in the end, if you'll pardon the expression. So much so that the chaps at the Church Centre began warning us of the grave dangers we were risking. They printed some strange notices that ran along the same lines as 19th century pamphlets about the horrors that could happen to boys who indulged in solo lechery. They actually gave a list of the foul symptoms that could follow on the Ouija board. It, or any stop-gap such as an inverted glass, was as good as inviting a demonic presence to squat in the soul. One could fall into raving madness or even drop dead on the instant.

They did not know their students. With the lodgings that some of them lived in, total insanity could seem like a pleasant change! As for instant death: "Better than a slow one" was their murky riposte. The crusade by these amateur social workers

---

3. Extra-sensory perception, e.g. clairvoyance, telepathy, psycho-kinesis and pre-cognition.

brought us more new members than either the Kung Fu Club or the Young Black Shirts!

We've all seen Catholic exorcism in films like 'The Ipswich Witch' or 'The Nuneaton Nun', but you haven't lived till you've beheld the Anglican variety. The Papists tee off with the same zeal as men selling stamps in the Post Office. They are casual as your average plumber when he comes to repair a leak. Their speech though is slick. They used to be fast in Latin, but in their native tongue they zip through it like shop stewards.

One can only surmise that the devil's sense of hearing is fixed at the same pitch as a berserk whippet. You are still looking for the place in the book and he's waltzing off with the choir-boy. You thought he'd been clearing his throat or warring with a little touch of asthma, but no - that was it. He came, he saw, he's off to the next one! He does it all so dead-pan too. He makes it clear that he's only doing his job and no offence intended.

In actual fact of course, he belie~es that it is the words themselves that count. It is best to keep emotions out of it. According to his creed, it has nothing to do with what he does, and depends on God sticking his nose in. Words are scattered at random like mustard seed on good ground or on stones. He slings his formulae over his shoulder with all the care of notes in bottles sailing out to sea.

One doesn't know if he uttered the secret name of God or whether he hurled it like a harpoon. He enjoins the great white whale to come to heel. He tries to tame Behemoth with holy water, and to wrap Babylon in chains of gabbled prayer. And when he went, did Ahab smile with triumph? Nobody knows.

Exorcism New

The Anglican puts on more of a show and invests all of his talent. His church is not sure about the reality of the devil so there has to be more of a performance. It is far more graphic, not to say epic, as if an Academy Award were on the horizon. During the sixties, there was a great craze for these things. The press went to town with inside stories, exposés and pictures that were going to shock the world. All the media were touched by the fashion and churned out such titbits as 'The Evil in our Midst', or 'The Devil Resides in a Caravan Café'. They knew a good story when they saw one.

I remember watching the eyes of a parson as he tussled with a devil that had taken up lodgings in a pretty woman. He was a meaty man who had lived on more than curate's eggs! He shook with passion. Nay, he even wobbled with it. His eye kept inching to the camera, while the frantic victim frothed at the mouth and inched her chair to a more central spot. He was so stirred by the Holy Spirit that he quite forgot his words and covered up with rabid gesture. The liturgy lapsed as he gnashed his false teeth with pluck and trotted through a long litany of eldritch animal noises.

It was quite obvious to all the viewers that the diabolic spirit had now passed into him. The one-time victim felt outdone and was not going to have this at all. She could see her film career being filched before her eyes. Purged of all evil in an instant, she tried to exorcise the vicar by belting him round the head with her handbag. The manager made a quick cut to the weather studio where a poor sod was caught without his wig, knitting a windsock.

This veneer of piety has a rather vicious side too, for one can detect something which wants to display its massive power. True, some people snigger, some are excited, but many are left with a sense of rising terror. In addition to which there's that little bit extra which boosts falling figures for presence in church on Sundays - and does it for wrong reasons. My father did not much approve of any of this and he told them so quite candidly.

"If God, one of the defunct spirits, or any denizen of the Beyond wished to cross the barrier, he already has the means of doing so without any fuss or clamour. It is not for us to order them. It would be sheer arrogance on our part to try and issue commands."

"Imagine, if you will, a rainy night in hell. It is one of the special pavilions, sited on an iceberg, and reserved for the wicked who hail from lands close to the equator. Just to add to their torment, the devil has ordered that the boiler be turned down. You can just picture it, can't you?"

"Then, all of a sudden, a call comes through from a seance being held in a liberal salon. 'If there is anybody there,' flutes a maidenly voice, 'we conjure thee to come to us.' The grins of the damned all freeze. 'Let me go,' begs one. 'It's my turn,' hisses a second. The third winds up his mouth corners. 'Sorry, boys. I'm feeling peckish!'"

"Like a warm candle, his face changes. His features run and the grotesque teeth and snout look more and more vulpine. 'I'll bring back presents,' comes the echo as he whispers off to the party."

Contact with Aleister

What AC was driving at was the fact that we have no mandate! By what right do we trespass in that other world? By what authority do we meddle with the laws of the cosmos? Yet we go on abusing the rules and hurting the natural order as if we were born with some ancestral title. As Nietzsche said: At the base of all these aristocratic races the predator is not to be mistaken, the splendorous *blond beast*, avidly rampant for plunder and victory.

Yes, it is just, faintly possible that one of us has been given the licence, or that the other world summons him. But you should also remember that access to The Beyond is always possible by means of magic. Be careful though! Don't just swagger forth as naked as David, using your jock-strap as a sling.

"Just as the rose is a potential that resides in every seed," Aleister told me, "so the '*chances of being perfect*' persist in every life."

"We do not come," he went on, "as aliens into this world, but as friends already loving it. If we grow and fulfil our promise then we belong on both sides of the veil." His voice fell a tone and he spoke sadly. "But because of the constant arousal of our senses, we respect what we see in the mirror."

For these reasons, I was not exactly waiting with bated breath for a spirit message from beyond the grave or, in Crowley's case, from the back of the chimney. He was fully equipped, and the lines of contact had been in existence for aeons. The only snag was: had I been given a telephone? Neither the gods nor anyone else is going to go outside the system - not even to tell you that the Day of Doom is nigh. There would be no point! What could we do? Anyway, when he died, I felt that he would contact me if it were at all possible.

And he has done so. Yes, he has proved me right. Putting it with a certain sense of irony, AC has been in touch! He speaks to me. He has spoken through me. And perhaps the most interesting of all, people have seen the two of us, ambling along a country lane, heads bent together in deep discussion. Now, I

90

have to say straight out that, myself, I'm not too conscious of this. Usually, I have no memory and rely on others to say. The strange thing is, it happens more often as I grow older. By the time I'm seventy, this may be his address more often than mine. Would that make me a lunatic, I ask?

In fact, not only does he contact me, but also any person who happens to be - er - dear to my heart. It's not as though I've taken any vows, you see. What I'm trying to say is, I don't exactly live the life of a monk. Not that monks are any better than they should be ... or at least, not the ones I've met. But that's another story.

Well, I'm not sure what effect Aleister Crowley had on his own bed-mates - but he delivers one hell of a shock to mine! I have known some of them hit the ceiling, AND they insisted on staying there. Others have vaulted through the open window only to get netted by the Virginia Creeper, or trapped in the cucumber frame.

I don't get cross with either party - him or them. I mean to say, how could I? It isn't anger that is called for so much as a little bit of tact. It does wonders for a wilting libido to be bedded by the son, and then chatted up by the paternal ghost. One must show them some kind of sympathy or else they scream the house down.

Once they have gone - and one is tempted to add that more people go than actually come - how does their memory deal with events? Maybe they just dismiss it from their minds? Or do they assume that I was a gifted ventriloquist who had awfully long arms?

91

Figure 1.

EXORCISM

1. EVICTING A SQUATTER

A. FROM A LIVING ENTITY
(Whether aware or not)
The squatter is a living person.
The squatter is a dead person.
The squatter is an animal, dead or living.
The squatter is an entity from elsewhere.
The squatter arises from an auto-charge.
The charge has been raised by someone else.
The charge is an historic or antique one.

B. FROM INERT MATTER
(Whether wilful or chance, known or unknown)
A man-made object : doll, gris-gris, parchment etc.
A natural object : stone, feather, toad, rain etc.
A specific location : lake, well, rock, road etc.

2. UNBINDING A SPELL OR A CURSE

Intentional application of malefic wishes.
The 'Evil Eye' and similar unintentional effects.
The results of so-called ancestral curses and legends.
Sites of ancient temples, tombs, sacrifices etc.
Spells brought about by mental or emotional illness.
Spells due to misaligned sexual forces or activities.

3. PSYCHIC CLEANSING

Purging someone after exorcism or primary cause.
Diagnosis of an Intrusion, new or old, waxing or waning.
Build-up of negative charges due to sexual practices.
Build-up of emotive waste and by-products e.g., grief.

13

ASTARTE

Ashtoreth or Ishtar, goddess of fields of battle

Two Females

AC's presence was very strong when I was writing and then trying to publish the first book. There was one young lady to whom he took a particular dislike. When I say young, she was walking without sticks, and when I say lady, she was not yet shaving. She was neither a Mrs (as in Mississippi) nor a Miss (as in mistake), but just a plain Miz (as in: 'T'is a Pity She's a Whore'). Does one call her 'she' or is that sexist? It might be more fitting to refer to 'It,' or 'thing'.

My father likened her to a very old chest of drawers - "far too stressed to be all that genuine"! In any case, she did me great wrong. I must not disclose what that wrong was since it might identify her too closely. She stole from me. It was a bit more grave than simple larceny, alas. I put my faith in her and she betrayed my trust. She knows she was in the wrong because she panicked and then tried to threaten me. She did not so much as mention the wrong she had done, much less apologise. She has not repaid the debt in the year and a day allowed, so I am no longer barred from acting. Neither is my father. Nor are my 'guardians' from Beyond. The lady has smugly opened the door.

The matter could well have been the subject of a lawsuit. I sought legal opinion and was told I had a very good case, chiefly since the lady could influence others against me, and seems to have done so. But where is the point of taking things to court since? Why go public? I took advice to make sure that I wasn't just blinded by anger. I shall seek justice elsewhere. My father said he'll attend to it. He's very good like that.

While speaking of things that leave a nasty taste, I must say plainly that I am not generally in favour of spirit seances. Yes I can feel for the genuine believer, but there is too much room for trickery and fraud. Over the years, there have been too many exposures of false mediums or cheats. They are in trade all over the world, not least in Europe and America. When my students get involved, and it does happen, I advise them to ponder some of the possible outcomes.

The matter is always covered in the lessons one gives a beginner just to cool his ardour. I explain to them that ninety six per cent of all psychic events can be explained by other means. Yet there remains that four per cent of events where something eerie is at work. At odds of twenty-four to one, no betting man is going to take a risk. You must weigh the chances of winning against the risks of losing and, frankly, it just isn't worth it.

As I said before, Aleister Crowley has been in touch with me. Teasing him a little, and to pose a small test, I suggested that he contact 'The Man in the Iron Mask' and ask him some telling questions. Back came a reply that quite dismayed us: "Why do you think it was a man?" That could only be my father! But behind those eight words, you see, there is something very secret.

People have been trying to guess for centuries who that famous prisoner could have been. It's so obvious, one overlooks it: 'The Man in the Iron Mask' was a woman. No, she was not just someone taking a new kind of beauty treatment or dealing with enlarged pores. This was someone very important to the King - and someone too close to kill. Aleister Crowley seems to have grounds for believing that it was the King's real mother.

America

Crowley was no stranger to the New World and he often spoke to me about his attitudes to the place and the people. I don't know for sure how many times he visited the country, but he had some good friends and a few established groups of followers. I, on the other hand, have never been to America. Much of what follows in this section is therefore based on my father's own views. When necessary, I have made his idiom more topical and changed the names of the people he cited.

The United States of America has brought about the biggest upheaval since Peter and Paul decided one to be front-man and the other the back-room boy of the church. Only they can speak of the country without a vague touch of contempt in their voice.

In its brief history, it has made itself the most disliked nation with the most loathed society in the world. In the realm of cinema, of course, no one else can touch them. Just think of such cultural gems as Donald Duck, Michael Jackson and Madonna!

Then think of all the great scientific leaps they have sold us: hamburgers, pop music, hot-dogs, drinks like Coca-cola and then tomato ketchup! Last but not least there is their own, special version of the English Language for which everyone blames Great Britain. All that and ageless women who go on looking like kewpie dolls even after they have died. Not to mention men, or 'studs' as they are called in a more tasteful TV programme, who look either like mutants or rejects from a rubber factory. This is the throw away, chewing gum culture of the New World. Columbus should have drowned!

Some folk do truly like America ... about half the people who live there, for example. I find it ominous that they are all so blind to their own defects. They are the only ones in the world who actually believe they are perfect. (The French *say* it, but I suspect it's for their own benefit. Or else it is a rare glimpse of Gallic humour!) It is typical of Americans to believe that they won both World Wars. This is why they are ashamed of the Vietnam war: *not the body count*, but because it's one they lost!

They see the world as waiting to be saved by the light that only Uncle Sam can provide. They have never known self-doubt. Ah well, we must learn to live with them, I suppose. As their own grammar lets them express it: they are not about to go away. By and large, they are also a very generous people. But they are also far too familiar for our personal comfort. This makes their good will all the more painful since no one likes being beholden to noisy braggarts. They tell you all about their session with their analyst[1] in every lurid detail - thus proving that the therapy was a flop. Somehow or other, tact never quite reached those shores.

Beliefs

One thing that we cannot fail to observe is that America exports *new beliefs* - the majority of which entail certain costs. It does rather seem that most of these sects milk their sheep for every penny they can get. When they say that they'll help the convert to share his load, little does one think that they are speaking of his

---

1. i.e., psycho-analyst.

wallet.

But we are beginning to learn slowly. Somewhere behind the scenes, or sailing on a yacht, there is usually a chief and one or two wives. They don't exactly live like holy hermits - more like the late President Marcos on his wife's birthday. A few of them have either gone to gaol or else fled America to avoid it. They are very devoted frauds!

Ah well, let's not play the pharisee. The same thing happens here, doesn't it? Under the guise of occultism, experts read your urine or seek guidance in the fluff of your navel. Are we not gullible too? Have you never once been diddled? There are beliefs in Europe that also draw money out of your pocket. If school history serves me well, it was the traffic in 'pardons' that turned Martin Luther's stomach.

Do please correct me if I'm wrong. But the odd miracle doesn't do any financial harm to either the church or the local community. No offence intended but I very much doubt if the town of Lourdes, or the diocese of Pau, has lost a great deal because of the visions of Saint Bernadette. Equally, if and when the Pope decides to shift the Vatican to Warsaw, I bet the Roman council let his tyres down! Excuse my asking but did Christ have second thoughts about Money Changers and Dove Sellers?

In spite of all this, America is the home of Quaker Oats and Mormons, as well as Christian Science, the Jehovah's Witnesses, and Dianetics.[2] There are many, many more. Each rivals the others in terms of reknown and success. It is awkward not to be unkind when the holiest subjects are handled as if they fell off the back of a lorry. Americans are exactly the kind of persons who, witless at getting "closer, my God, to thee", won't hesitate 'to haul God's ass' closer to them!

The cream of American society, by the way, are those who can trace their descent from the Pilgrim Fathers and their ship 'The Mayflower'. The remainder, the teeming millions, are just details in the refugee hot-pot, and even if wealthy, they don't possess *the blood* but have merely climbed from the ranks! Have you noticed how many tenants of The White House go to Ireland, to find a signed tomb or some family photos? It's worth a few million votes to drink Guinness and have some Irish blood in your veins.

2. Better known as Scientology.

Uniting the Mobs

I can fathom what all this means. They deny having a chip on the shoulder but they are starving for roots, pedigree, and a valid history. Tell them they are the biggest, the loudest, the winners or the champions and they purr like cats who drank the cream. They haven't got the modesty to question the praise nor the finesse to wear it quietly. As tourists, they shout as if they were rounding up cattle and bring blushes to the heavily made-up cheeks of the Ladies of the Night in Chelsea or the Pigalle. It might even please them to know they are the least popular visitors.

As a nation, the American people have two things in common. First, they all came from somewhere else and nobody tried to stop them leaving. Second, each came with his own faith, tongue and rules of hygiene. They had nothing which could bind them into one, so they went ahead and invented it: the federal state! Since then crime has done much the same thing and combined forces. It has aimed at police forces and made them corrupt. It has enmeshed men and women who work in top banks and in finance. It has even got tendrils in some very high places indeed. In short, America is not the land of freedom nor the home of heroes, but the crudest example of the dog eat dog outlook.

As one may gather, I do not like the United States. I hope very much the feeling is mutual because, as I said earlier, one may be judged by one's enemies. To be hated by Americans goes down well anywhere else in the world! If there is a Babylon then, as Kenneth Anger himself has pointed out, America could well be it. I would not go so far as to say that Uncle Sam is Satan. I merely notice how familiar his weird conduct seems!

Is this why their soil hatches more new religions per week than any other country in the world? The output and the income are almost as big as an industry. What with greed and no humility, any slight virtue is bound to be obscure. Not that I mind them making bespoke creeds. God knows, they quite likely need them. But I do wish they wouldn't try to convert. Having left the 'Old world' why are they so eager to bring us 'the message'? Is it belated revenge?

"Nor is it just churches, my dear, but occultism too!" When Aleister Crowley said this, it was almost a prophecy. Look at the ubiquity of A.M.O.R.C. - The American Order of the Rose

97

Croix. Think of the Mexican peyotl or sacred mushroom cults. Above all, let us not forget that something which they call paganism is usually a mix of drugs and witchery. As if this were not enough, there are also the animist religions of native Indian Tribes.

Scientology, as we all know by now, was the idea of a science fiction writer. Any newspaper can show you its archive on the subject. What very few of them bother to mention is that Ron Hubbard was once a student of Crowley ... for a time. Now Hubbard's friends may well claim that he saw the light and left. The brutal truth is that Crowley got rid of him.

"The man's moral outlook is not at all compatible with magick!" he declared. Imagine that, eh? That's quite something to have been rejected by the so-called "wickedest man in the world". Ah well, I don't blame them, these Yanks. To crib George Orwell, we all have the faith we deserve![3]

But for several years now, an important feature of the American way of life has been racial hatred, violence, and a ghastly rate of murder. Small wonder they wish to prove they are cultured! It went down very well indeed when Thor Heyerdahl showed that the sailors from Ancient Egypt could have voyaged to America - though he never explained why they would have done so. It went down even better when it was 'proved' that the 'real' Erik the Viking, otherwise known as Leif Eriksson, passed by that way.[4] But after having half wiped them out, Americans are now curious about native Indian beliefs.

Secret Societies?
In a free country, citizens have the right to mingle with each other and form whatever clubs and societies that they wish. You will notice that in many modern countries, England and France for instance, you may certainly go ahead and do this but full details must be put on the records. They can grant you some tax benefits, give you a grant, or sort out problems with insurance, etc. In other words, you are free - as long as they approve.

Who are 'they'? That is the question that wins the star prize. The ones who rule a country are the people with power. They hide in the shadows and allow a government to seem to rule us.

---

3. Entry in his MS notebook, 17 April, 1949: "At 50, everyone has the face he deserves."
4. The other Erik the Viking, the film by Monty Python, sank without trace.

They deceive the eye, dispel all doubt, and ward off any concern.

According to Fred Zeller[5], the French Head of State would have been left-wing in 1974 had not Valéry Giscard d'Estaing become a Mason. He was enrolled in the *Franklin Roosevelt Lodge*, Paris, and the Masonic system supported him at the polls.[6]

Anyone who wants to study secret societies is faced with one great and obvious problem, that the bloody things are secret! The reason for this secrecy is not at all hard to find. In spite of their exalted and often muddled titles, secret societies are normally one of two kinds:-

(1) they are the adult equivalent of teenage gangs, set up to create an elite.

(2) they are going to do something for which they expect to be attacked.

Now it is quite true that the Christian Church has always been a wee bit too sensitive about rivalry. From just about the day she was brought into existence, she has not once endured the existence of any deviance in doctrine or opinion. The church has used gaol, torture, and burning alive. It has made war against other states, and effaced thousands of good but simple citizens all in the name of church primacy.

Today, however, the church is no longer supreme. It is still quite evident that she does her best to meddle in world affairs but - the old girl has lost her looks and her power to seduce. So we cannot just explain the *secrecy* of secret societies by citing the church as their eternal enemy. There were the same kind of societies in places where the church had no influence, and topmost figures of the church have been members of secret societies too.

The real opponent is the current faction, that is to say: the small number of people who manage society, and milk it dry. If you explore a secret society, a hard thing to do, you'll often find that it embodies a threat to the current balance of politics. Indeed, however badly phrased, one of their primary aims has always been to change the system.

Secret societies differ in the way they are formed, who their

---

5. Who was Grand Master of the Grand Orient of France in the years 1971 and 1973.

6. One of the best books to expose Masonry has already been cited: Steven Knight, "The Brotherhood" 1983, Granada Publishing. This book is forbidden to all masons. They may not buy it or read it, and risk expulsion if they do so. Presumably they are not supposed to know about their own organization. Now that is a really secret society for you!

members are, and what they say they are working for. If one starts to classify them by any of these criteria one will very soon become confused and lose sight of the crucial thread that runs through all of them. The target is worldly power, and the reason is spiritual knowledge.

At this point I am afraid we must really chuck away any views or opinions we might have about their material goals. Certainly, there are criminal combines like 'The Mafia', 'The Cosa Nostra', 'The Comorra' and so on - who are bent on filling their coffers. But do not be blinded by the idealism of men who make films. Many of them have Italian links! But even in films that are harshly opposed to the Mafia, there is a certain amount of glamour that wrenches the male heart.

True, the poor may benefit from the presence of these elite groups. A 'patron' may pay for a child's education, 'the family' will arrange for a successful career etc. But who runs the patrons? Where sits the spider on this international web of organized crime? You'll notice, it goes without saying, that every Mafia leader receives full ritual service from the Church! You will also remember that there was a scandal linking the Vatican Bank with Mafia funds. There are none so blind as those who will not see!

Secret societies need funds in order to exert influence. If you want to win, you must first be invited to play. You have to be noticed, and you have to stick to the rules. Oh there are always funds available. They are gleaned from fees, tariffs, gifts, special services, sales of objects, bequests, tithes and trading.

It does no harm if you can offer government or power brokers something to help their ambition. They want votes, high scores in the polls, a hold over the enemy, and access to the media. Musicians, singers, actors and writers too - many have sold their soul to the devil.

Men in high places live under the sword of Damocles.

14

YAMM

The tyrant of the sea whose greed made other gods rebel

Strangers in the Night
At the time when I first met Aleister Crowley, I was at the stage when boys worship heroes. Mine was Flash Gordon. My father would have been more pleased if I'd gone for Emperor Ming, I think.

But my awareness of America was built up from 'Tom Sawyer', 'King Kong' and two comedians called 'Abbot and Costello'. This could explain a great deal about my character, I don't doubt. That, plus a mother who relived every epic moment of the silver screen, was the central element of my growing years.

All the same, what shocked my father most was not what American people said, or liked, or spoke. It was their conduct. "Wherever you go in the world, you feel among men, and you can make yourself understood. Not in America though. They speak a different kind of English even though they take so much pride in their English roots. But in actual fact, one would feel so much more at home with the penguins of Morocco.[1]"

He told me quite frankly. "I cannot abide their virulent egoism nor live with their behaviour in public. What they accept as normal, would be grounds for being certified insane in this country! One would be lodged in the nearest lunatic asylum."

"It is wrong to be too hard on them, of course. They are victims also. Oh yes, they are being abused but without even knowing it. If ever they decide to follow the path you must smack their spiritual bottoms. Then explain with care that the home of the gods is not in California."

---

1. I am afraid that this is one of his more obscure jokes. I can only think it is the notion of birds from the icy wastes being out of place in the Sahara Desert. Of course, he did know Morocco very well and there may have been more in this quip.

He was beginning to get into his stride now and made one or two sniffing or coughing noises.

"One great skill the Americans do have is selling themselves to others. They are the world's best braggarts! If ever you report these sayings," he added with foresight, "do not doctor them. They will be very proud and not at all offended."

I don't know about you, but myself - I always felt there was a great deal of truth in what my father said. But since his day, the Americans have become very good with computers. The Japanese have done their best to overtake them but this is not possible. The people of Nippon are not inventive. They have minds more like cameras. Anyway, when America sells its systems to both friendly and hostile countries - there are many things they forget to tell you.

What better place to hide an electronic bug[2] than in the middle of an electronic tangle where it would not be noticed? A TV set would do, to be sure, except that the noise of the programme would drown out everything else. The same could be said of a radio, of course.

But it may not be dialogue that most interests them. If they wish to learn about plans, designs, economy, bank deals and arms strategy then ... what better tool than a trusty computer?

Now not all computers come from America, to be sure. But in most people's eyes, the best ones do. The other builders - Taiwan, Korea, Japan etc - all make copies and are very proud indeed to announce the fact. The one, single, most vital word of all is: compatible. The standard is set by American companies and then the rest of the world does its very best to match that standard as quickly as it possibly can.

When you think about it, this is just another way of saying that the innards work the same way, that they have identical 'chips'. I am told that the proper term is: "they have the same architecture".

What crept into the crypt
Oh people of Israel, do ye sleep safely in your tents? And you, all the children of Arabia, are you rubbing your hands with glee? Have you all bought bargains in Bulgaria? And all you smug Europeans - England, France, Germany and the rest - do you feel so safe in your new alliance? What about the individual men and

---

2. A miniature gadget that can transmit speech, or eavesdrop on the information put into a computer.

women, the private citizens, who own a computer - are you quite safe too? You have heard about viruses and worms? You have made use of pirated copies of expensive programs? Ah, well, think about your position and the risks you are taking. Do you realize *how much they know about you?*

You may even nurse the false impression that you are guarded from all misdeed or disorder if your computer has no direct contact with the outer world. But I suppose you plug in to the normal electricity supply? And you know all about the intercom or the 'baby listener' which also use the mains wiring as a means of communication?

Do you, by any chance, also have a nice, shiny telephone? Do your savings run to a television set with your own aerial on the roof? Oh goodness me! Don't tell me you've even got a satellite dish? Well - there you are! The means exist! If anyone wanted, they could spy on you, steal from you or even ruin you. It's like having a ghost inside your house or office, or an evil presence that needs to be exorcized.

In any case, when a computer is working, it emits signals that radiate outward around the building. Unless the room is in a Faraday cage[3], industrial spies or foreign agents should be able to 'pick up' and 'read' all activities.

As above, so below! That's how the ancient saying goes, isn't it? For what the news is worth, it is the guiding ethos of the Freemasons too. In addition to which there is that charming theory to do with the grand Macrocosm and the puny Microcosm. I am turning your eye to see a new idea.

The gap between modern science and ancient magic is neither as wide nor as deep as we think. One is achieved by trust in our own headway, and the other by credence in the world beyond here and now. New found powers or vintage forces, what does it matter? You can be killed by the unknown just as easily as by a syringe hidden in an umbrella.

Imagine what could be done over space and time if we used occult or magical means. If you trusted such things, you'd realise what was taking place, and you'd be able to take some counter measures. On the other hand, if the magical system is foreign to you - let's say Mexican, or one based on ancient Apache beliefs - then you are in a pickle. Worse still, if you are a total sceptic, as

---

3.   An earthed metal screen which excludes electrostatic influence.

were all the experts about AIDS, then you might succumb.

You do know what the letters CIA stand for? And you know that GM means Grand Master. Put one with the other and you have an anagram for MAGIC. As the old Countess said in Pushkin's story, The 'Queen of Spades': "Too late now!"

Bradford & Oxford

An old friend of my father was an auditor who lived in Bradford. When I was a child, I went there once or twice to watch them play Rugby League. It was a typical Northern city whose wealth came from wool and it had two theatres, one renowned for its Christmas shows.

The auditor was a fairly important man who owned stock in a local newspaper called 'The Telegraph and Argus'! He was also the head of a country branch of The Hermetic Order of the Golden Dawn. This unique off-shoot achieved great fame in occult circles. In the first place, it was larger than the parent group. In the second, it went on working long after the other had tumbled and vanished. It was no doubt helped by the number of local worthies who acted as its officers. There were owners of large mills, bankers, some very rich men of business, chaps who built department stores and traders.

As a matter of curiosity, there was also someone who worked for the Bishop of Bradford. It was a Bishop of Bradford whose harsh sermons were later to add pressure to the outcry against King Edward VIII. His diatribes from the pulpit tied the hands of the British government and lent weight to the clamour for the King to abdicate. Now I know of no link but, as I explain later, the Freemasons had a very strong interest in getting Mrs Wallis Simpson on to the throne. So there you are, you see? It is one of those obscure little facts which grows more and more significant as you think about it.

This is purely my own opinion but I think a sort of war was played out in Bradford in those years. The Freemason faction who wanted to keep the King on the throne, and the occult faction who deemed him unworthy of the role. I also know that certain individuals were members of both sides - and no one could ever be really sure where these men were at home and where they did their spying. One thing is sure, there was a lot of chopping and changing in the world of business affairs round about that period. One or two careers were badly blasted and a few were very well launched.

I have often wondered whether there still is an active occult group in that city environs. I do know for certain that there are fully active 'besom pilots'[4] in the commuter zones of Idle, Keighley, Bingley, Brighouse, Pudsey and even the home town of the Bronte sisters at Haworth. How can I be so sure? Well, I have friends - and they don't do much to hide it actually. There have been letters. They have written to me to ask more about the 'gateways' that A.C. built when he wrote the rituals for Gardner.

What with one thing and another, it's quite a lively place, is Bradford!

I say all this to show that this auditor was a man of some influence. At a suitable time, about 1950, he wrote to the Warden of one of the Oxford colleges and recommended me. The outcome was that they invited me to visit the college and to lunch at High Table. He was an extremely charming man who could not have been more kind. I think he could see how nervous I was and managed to put me at ease. I imagine this is an essential skill for a man in his position. It was at the end of lunch that he offered me a place to read English. It was a little later, while we were taking brandy in his lodging, that I turned the offer down.

Naturally, I did my best to give my reasons. It was no good my accepting just out of gratitude, I said. He had done his best to make me feel welcome, and I had indeed felt very welcome. But I had not felt at home. I found the college even more august than my old grammar school, and I reckoned that I might respond badly and be miserable. I could see by his face that he was very shocked. Quite honestly, I don't think he felt that he had done me some great honour for which I should have been more grateful. He seemed genuinely sad for me, as if he thought I would regret it. As indeed I did.

I said that it would be better if I went to a red-brick university - one of those civic ventures whose standing had recently been raised to meet post-war demand for education. The Warden was not annoyed though I had wasted some of his time and some of my own money. He hoped I'd do well and not rue my rashness. Me too! I knew my reasons were all wrong, but I also felt that I

4. i.e. broomstick riders, or witches.

would never overcome my hatred of snobbery. At the time, I did not realize that I had become one myself. But then, as Aleister once put it: "some people are more perfect than others!"[5]

Je ne sais quoi

To be fair to my own talents though, this and other choices in my life always have seemed to be 'out of my hands'. You may be quite sure that I weighed up all the options, but I suppose I was trained by quite a harsh teacher. Plainly, no matter where I'd gone or whatever decision I'd made, there would have been the same kind of outcome. It is no good asking if things would have been different! Do your Edith Piaff spoof and have no regrets. If you work in harmony with your finest impulse you'll wind your way toward your true destiny.

I am that which I am. I do that which I do. I am here, and now, because that is right for everybody. All along the way, there were choices which had to be made. I was (*one is*) quite free to react according to my (*one's*) will. The virtues of Will - its flavour, perfume, and quality - are due entirely to life, plus a sprinkle of the Chef's *'je ne sais quoi'*. I can taste it. I can eat it. I can even snuffle it like my dog. Then it becomes the whole object of my life to discover what it is, this *'je ne sais quoi'*.

You'll find it easily if you look, despite the wrong turnings in the maze.

At the present moment, Paris has some very complex rules about who is French or not. But under common market rules, any European will soon be able to vote in France. This has cooled their ardour. It means they would have to change the constitution. The people who mocked at England's fears are having one or two of their own now. As things stood, a child born of foreign parents on French soil could ask for a French passport as long as he did his military service. The same used to be true in England too.

I was made close to Boulogne. My father's poor sperm had to swim through bubbles of champagne with all the zest of Tarzan. But that does not count. Very little counts in France. I am one of those funny, tainted persons from across La Manche. I come from a country that beat the great Napoleon, they say, by sheer

---

5. This was a reference to 'Animal Farm', once again by George Orwell. Since the book wasn't written until 1945, this is odd to say the least.

good luck and stealth. This is why, even when talking about a rugby match between the two countries, French Television always refers to *"la perfide Albion"*.[6] You might think it's a joke at first. But it isn't. They repeat it, over and over again.

Heraldic Beasts

They have a tendency, the French, to relieve their tensions and complexes in what has been called "Gallic Wit". That is why their last Emperor and Empress are buried in England[7], where they fled to escape their loyal subjects. You've all heard about French farmers who burn lorries of British lamb or spray them with paint. They do the same thing with cargoes of onions, or anything else they take objection to. They even threaten the lives of any French person who works for the shipping company or owns a lorry.

When the French speak of the European Spirit, doesn't it all ring a bit hollow? It is so instructive to hear them lecture the English on sincerity, as they form a joint army with Germany. Is this why the two countries are all but ready to announce their marriage? Imagine what the European Community would be like if it were dominated by the joint economic powers of those two great countries.

The biggest puzzle of all, the one that baffles the French completely, is the fact that the English actually like them. But then, you see, some of their land is sacred to us. We *have many armies of dead soldiers lying there.* Our two histories have been closely twined and our blood has both mingled and spilled together. One need only study the heraldic symbols of our various noble families. One need only interpret the true significance of some of the strange, heraldic beasts.

But the world of politics is not really the issue for a true occultist. So why do I let myself be so drawn on the subject? Ah well, you see, there are secret societies behind it all. To be specific, there are groups who are very keen to obtain and manipulate worldly power. This is one reason why their agents make such big mistakes when dealing with me: they cannot believe that I have a different set of motives.

---

6. "Attaquons dans ses eaux La perfide Albion!" [Let us attack her in her own waters perfidious Albion!] Augustin, Marquis de Ximénez, 1726 - 1817.
7. In Farnborough Abbey, Hampshire, which the Empress Eugenie endowed as a monastery.

But the occultists of France must know, must be aware of, must even share - the ambitions of parallel occult groups in Germany and Switzerland?

I pass through all these countries. I am, if you like, something of a perpetual tourist. But no matter where I go, friends arrange things - hotels, meetings and travel. I even meet some other occultists who have no connection with me or my groups. But we regard each other with mutual respect and no mistrust at all.

What with one thing and another, I have quite a good vantage point over the occult world. I make it my business to know what's afoot and where it's happening. No, this is a little more serious than chit-chat or gossip. After all, there are certain facts that have to be faced. I am quite taken with the idea of staying alive and, if possible, intact. That gives me a very good reason for keeping my eyes open.

So, in case you didn't know, dear reader, an ancient evil is uncoiling again in the world. The Angel of Death is mustering thousands of part-time staff and the Green Dragon is unfolding its wings.

15

MENAT

The necklace shaken by the priestess of Hathor

Deaths of Princes

Elected leaders are never anointed. They just swear them in, or launch them like life-boats! While in office they gather no aura, no mystique, and there is no sense of their being sacred. They are Heads of State, like Kings, except they were chosen by the vox populi. Their job is to act as 'first citizen'. The problem is that people who didn't vote for him, must also accept him. But they don't. They resent his being imposed on them. He is not their choice. Thus a President lives in danger. Far from being loved by all, he is hated by about half the population.

Further, a President is in the limelight more than any King would be. His seat is more obvious. Royalty lives two lives. First: the state one, which is a series of rituals performed with dignity and composure. Second: the private one, which is usually veiled from public view.

Until recently, the right to privacy was respected. Society knew how hard it would be to keep a state stable if the ruler's human frailties were exposed. This is the reason for court protocol. Monarchs do not show emotion in public. People need them to be part of a living myth. How else can we explain the genuine love in which they are held? A nation grieves when its King dies yet very few have ever met him.

Presidents, on the other hand, are obliged to expose their private life in the minutest detail, short of actual indecency. They must live by the same rules as everyone else because the populace expect the first family to epitomize all the traditional values of the state. Thus, when a President is ill, the television crews close up on his vomiting. When President J.F.Kennedy was murdered, it was judged appropriate and proper for the television news to show the top of the poor man's skull being shot off.

An earlier president, who was called Franklin D. Roosevelt did all in his power to hide the fact that his legs were severely crippled by polio. He could be filmed standing. He could be filmed walking. But scarcely anyone ever got pictures of him being wheeled about in his special chair.

The ways in which one can become President differ from one republic to another. But whatever they might be, the way is open for someone to make himself eligible even when he has secret motives for doing so. Now it is no great secret that the first President of the United States, George Washington, was a member of the Freemasons. The same statement holds true for many of those who followed. The great seal bears masonic symbols, and even the humble dollar looks like a masonic credit card.

But John F. Kennedy was not a Freemason. The family is of Irish descent, and they are all devout Catholics. The Vatican has been unkind to Masons for years. This is because members of its own hierarchy have been, and still are, members. Pope Leo XIII in his encyclical Humanus Genus (1884) put Masons "in the kingdom of Satan".

A canon law of 1917 said that any Catholic who became a Freemason was *ipso facto* expelled from the church.[1] President Kennedy was shot. So were members of his family who sought power or whose ambitions aimed too high.

Other American presidents have also been murdered, and so have presidents in other parts of the world. When Kings have been killed, it was usually by some other claimant to the throne. Presidents are rarely killed by just one individual who has become sick. It is usually by some group which sees its own position being threatened. It may believe that its own interests are best served if the President goes.

Oh yes. The poor culprit who has been persuaded to fire the fatal shot or toss the bomb, is often some wretch with a history of mental illness. But these are scapegoats. These are mere dupes. I have no special link with any centre of learning, but perhaps one

---

1. One does not forbid little boys to steal apples unless little boys show a distinct tendency to do so. Neither does a church threaten its own members who become Freemasons unless those members have been doing so. There is powerful evidence, e.g., the infamous P2 Lodge in Italy, that high-ranking church members have long been involved.

of them might care to probe these matters more deeply? They might also look for a link between Masonry and Bolshevism, since the old regime had been very deeply penetrated.

I am assuming, of course, that the academic staff of a university are neutral, as all good scholars should be. But there are grounds for thinking otherwise. Some members of Faculty are known for their left-wing or even anarchist views. It is no good asking them to own up, is it? They are very happy where they are - bending the minds of the young.

My father was very fond of the mystic Russian known as Grigori Rasputin. This same Rasputin was trying to lead the Tsar away from War and the international struggle for power. One might be curious about the man who murdered him, Prince Yusupov, and ask if he was one *the brethren*?[2]

The Ones in the Know

But if some people are blessed with good fortune, we must notice that others seem cursed with bad fortune. They certainly think so at any rate, and they are the ones who stand closest to the problem. They seem to recognize that the cards are stacked against them from birth. They have no doubt at all that the dice are loaded.

As you might expect, this does not exactly aid their concentration. Neither does it do much to boost their sense of personal ambition. How can we interest them in the game if they know they are destined to lose? It isn't good for their morale, you see. It makes them apathetic.

You can see why someone like that notices the weeds and misses the flowers. He looks to the sky but sees clouds on the horizon instead of sun above his head. To his eyes, the colour grey is observed as 'light black' and never as 'dark white'. Every object casts a long shadow. All beauty endures for only a day. He is gloomy by nature now, and any shafts of revelatory truth will simply bounce off him. His soul is armoured against hope. The very jelly of his eyes has changed colour.

People like this quickly become obsessed by morbid thoughts.

2. The way that history has treated Rasputin is not a hundred miles away from the way they treated my father. The same ingredients are there: sexual excesses, total amorality, hypnotic influence over the Tsarina, the power to cure the haemophiliac Tsarevich, and the (reported) widespread hate.

They begin to smell intrigue where there isn't any. They look for treason where it never existed. Their friends begin to worry. Is it a case for Crocodile Dundee, or do they send him to that other mental expert from Australia, Dr Fried?[3] These people are now deluded. They are lost in a fantasy. It is hard to speak with them because their language does not mean the same as ours. They can no longer tell the difference between the dream and the reality. They have been swallowed by unreason.

That is when the big world makes the great big assumption that it's values are right and his are wrong. He is a minority, when all is said and done. But is it your logic which tells you that the majority is always right? Has there never once been a case where one, single man knew better?

This is the dilemma which confronts the fevered soul: "What if I am right after all? What if they are blind and I am the only one who can see?" Well, what would you do in such circumstances? Would you go along with the lemmings? Or would you let yourself be crucified? After all, it is just possible that the rest of the world is sick!

Royalty, of course, can rise above the rules. Noble birth brings perks which often include the right to dodge the nastier aspects of life. But we will find that the word 'noble' is derived from 'gnosis', which means 'knowledge'.

Around the king there was a small group of men who guarded him from everything except - his duty to die. Hence there is a minority of persons who try to cocoon themselves out of reach of tragedy. They take out insurance, they build secret passages, they swear loyalty to strange masters. In brief, they try to disown and therefore shed an important part of their humanity. Like the fools depicted in the book 'The Decameron' by Bocaccio[4], they lock themselves in the castle and hope that the plague will pass the gates.

Does nobility count over there? Do spirits speak in a Mayfair accent? Does grouse-shooting, Ascot or Henley matter a damn to the gods? They are unaware that the "gels" of Africa are dying for want of smoked salmon sandwiches. They stay aloof from the world, out of touch with reality. They preen like peacocks, not

3. Dr Freud from Austria!
4. This famous book is a catalogue of cautionary and risqué tales that courtiers are supposed to have told one another as they tried to outlive the plague, locked in their palace.

realizing they they are the inmates of a velvet Bedlam.

At some point back in time, an ancestor was a trollop who got the royal wink. The true origins of the Order of the Garter! Or else a chap backed the winning side, chopped up a few thousand soldiers, and got the blue blood through spilling vast volumes of red. The nobility are the product of a ruthless greed that is called the Divine Right of Kings in one epoch, a Police State in another, and a Democratic Republic in a third. But cheer up, my friends. Don't forget the obscure law of Euclid: "The Higher they climb, the harder they'll fall".

The Ultimate Gift

Since humans first arrived on earth, we have made and unmade gods by the thousand. One tribe was conquered by another and their gods were displaced by the new arrivals. But it was mostly a matter of names. "However you address me," said each God, "I shall know that you mean Me." That made no difference though. As man's society changed, so his pantheon changed in step. Gods have worn togas, Byzantine robes, suits or T-shirts and jeans. They are ours to dress as we wish. You want a monster? Then here is Moloch! You'd like a meek Shepherd? Then have a 19th century Christ. Whatever the truth might be, you will paint it to suit.

Well, it is a fact that we can detect broad patterns in the onward march of religion. He may be deeply pious but man is prone to criticize. His inner wishes slowly change one reality into another one. This is why the old gods went. Neither we nor they were useful to one another, and they had no intention of scrapping the experiment before it had run its course. While we are busy judging them, they too are measuring us. A man looks at a religion and asks himself totally the wrong question: "Do I like it?" The gods look at you and they ask: "Will he do?"

Fashions change but the truth is constant. Religions rise and fall, but the original Gods stay put. We speak of battles between the Titans but though old gods, *chthonic* gods, were toppled in our esteem - they were never killed. Where do they go then? Do they just vanish? Do they take a courtly bow as they leave the stage, never to be seen again? Like the pet-meat factory for scraggy horses, and the garbage dump for domestic waste ... is there a dust-bin or slag-heap for the gods that Men have finished with?

113

Are holy beings re-cycled or broken up as spare parts?

If we go back far enough in time, we find that people believed they must make an offering to God or the Gods. It is so common today always to construe that word 'sacrifice' as if it were the same as 'carnage'. In fact it means to make holy, or to connect with the sacred. Even the term 'a living sacrifice' might not mean what you suppose. The Roman Emperor, Heliogabalus (218 - 222)[5], was dominant High Priest of the Syrian god, Gabal.[6] Within the temple there was a huge rounded stone, not unlike a tower with a dome on top. Male devotees could mount a gallery in order to masturbate, or be masturbated, and they spent their discharge onto the sacred stone.

Over the years, the outward appearance of the stone must have been quite grotesque. But the fabric of the stone had also absorbed an immense quantity of *male force*, or *father force*. In this way, the orgasm was seen as a free-will offering to the God represented by the stone. That stone was itself planted in the body of the Earth which represented the eternal mother of all.

Now here is an odd thing that parallels one of the facts of modern occultism. *An orgasm that was achieved without the aid of erotic fantasy of any kind was considered to be more noble still.* The purer the mind, the more glorious and worthy the gift became. Or, to put it more vividly: tootling your flute by ear was nicer than playing an old melody.

The Spirit Conforms

The word 'royal' comes from a Latin word regalis. The word 'real' comes from another Latin word, realis. In antique times, these had one and the same meaning. They both meant *true, right, proper* or *fitting*. I mention this because it is the prime goal of any student of magic to learn what is royal or real.

This is how the quest for the Holy Grail (or Saint Graal) replaced the original search for the "*sang réal*" i.e., the proper blood, or the road to entelechy. The modern magus should be engaged on this ancient quest. A Master, like a professor, can direct his studies but only the person himself is able to see, hear

---

5. There is a superb painting by the English Artist, Alma Tadema, called "The Banquet of Heliogabalus". In the real event the guests were showered with clouds of rose petals until they all suffocated - presumably in ecstasy.

6. This is Baal in his solar aspect, as "swallower" of the sun. There is a superb temple still extant in the Syrian town of Homs.

and recognize the change. The vision has to be a private one.

To achieve this, the magician regards 'loss of self' or 'retreat from self' as a step to be welcomed. He stops trying to maintain his own unique identity and allows himself to merge into, and become one with, one other - many others - and finally with All. To be sure, concepts of this type are rare and elusive. They are not the kind of thing that ordinary people talk about every day. Hence, many individuals are put off, or left behind. The sheer expertise of a guide can make the students abandon the path. This is where the mystic quality of love comes in.

If you identify with, and are no different from, God then you can rise above the bonds of birth, death and mere material existence. One must have grown into God to achieve this. One has no need to be 'saved' or 'damned'. One needs to be taught how the alchemy is done. One does not go to a 'heaven' in the sky nor yet to a 'hell' in the earth. The one is not a paradise of cream cakes, bubbly and bodies. The other is not a sort of molten golf course where devils make your balls jump out of the holes, so to speak.

One joins oneself to nothing, or to all. One aligns with truth or lies. One sticks to the material level to wait for the end, or one steps aside and says: "I'm not involved. I'm free."

Will the heir mount the throne at the right time? Will he take on his ancient duties, as well as his modern ones? Shall it be him - or will something strange happen between now and then? For instance, shall the book fall open at a different page? The hierarchy will not know what to do. They'll be strumming a guitar for some 'with it' ritual.

16
SETH

The god who killed his brother, Osiris

Royalty

To foreign eyes, the most English thing about England is our royalty. To be sure, the French are intrigued by Royalty. It's almost as if they regretted having murdered their own.

All the same, it's hard to understand what they see in ours. So many of them know less about ordinary life than did Marie Antoinette. They travel about in de-luxe cars, hidden by minders of all kinds. It's not Ford Fiestas, Ferries or Virgin Airlines for them, mate; it's Rolls Royces, the Royal Yacht and the Queen's Flight. It might do them good to learn what it is like being without work.

Yes, they visit injured soldiers and drop in at sites of calamity, and one thinks them so kind. They are advised what to do in order to stay popular and so ward off any revolution. The Queen of England is one of the most wealthy people in the world. A single day's interest from her post office savings bank would go quite a long way to solving the country's social problems.

But when it was suggested that she should pay tax, a palace spokesman said Her Majesty would be happy to agree though, of course, she might have to sell Balmoral Castle. The matter was dropped. People sent in gifts of eggs and sliced-bread, just to keep her strength up.

But Royalty are faced with a career hazard. If you do sit on the throne, then some ill-bred persons will try to shoot you off it. There are attempts on one's life! This is why the palaces are big, and why the Royal bedrooms are put at the back. The spectre of death wanders along those gilded corridors and, of course, royal purple used to symbolize the supreme sacrifice that would follow. History's pages are wet with regal blood.

Check the facts. On some rainy Sunday, get your big books out and find out how many royals have died unnatural and violent deaths in the last hundred years. I packed it in when I got to fifty. One wonders if they can be insured and, if so, what kind of premiums must they pay? I don't wish to be vulgar but one has to be practical. Have you ever worked out how much a state funeral costs?

Why are they such popular targets? Well, not because they have any political power! That might be the case in sandy spots but even there, most kings have been deposed by mentally unstable army officers. These 'new' Heads of State, reeking of petrol, keep a private army between themselves and their own people.

No doubt about it, I'm afraid. Kings do still attract the eye of death because they are still 'The Chosen One', or the eldest son of the nation. Kingship began[1] as the best biscuit in the box! The purest, the most handsome, the most virile.

Criteria have changed since those days. But the customs remain the same and a golden circlet still marks the head which has been promised to the Gods. Once upon a time the King was the country. Kill him and you won the war, just as today you would win the game of chess. It is only recently that they were turned into robots or mere ritual symbols. In the recent past they were rendered sacred by being anointed with magic oils[2].

The Uncrowned King

As it happens, the British King named Edward VIII was never crowned and therefore never anointed with these magic oils. I need hardly remind you that, as Prince of Wales, he was enamoured of Mrs Wallis Simpson. When King George V died, he mounted the throne but was soon forced to abdicate by pressure from the establishment - not least from the Church of England. Edward VIII quite simply refused to end his affair with Mrs Simpson.

The Duke of York was next in line to the throne, and he became King George VI. He and his family did not truly

---

1. cf. 'The Golden Bough', Sir Gordon Frazer, MacMillan, 1922
2. Interestingly, there is a remnant of this in the English coronation ceremony. The monarch is clothed in a dalmatic, covered by a canopy, and anointed with "holy oils". People think that this is intended to "ordain" the monarch as the Head of the Church of England. But in fact the rite existed long before the separation from Rome.

welcome the job, and found it impossible to forgive the elder brother. What is not so well known is that the ex-King never forgave them either. During the crisis, only his younger brother, The Duke of Kent, had given any moral support. He was very bitter about this. After the events, he expected a show of affection and understanding. He didn't get it.

The new King, George VI, realized it would be an impossible situation to have the ex-King dashing round London or dropping in at court. So he banished him, and gave him the title Duke of Windsor together with a stipend. There was a strict condition that the ex-King and his wife would never be so foolish as to have any children. This would only aggravate an already grave crisis. So far as anyone knows, this proviso was followed to the letter.

The Duke of Windsor was not present when his brother was crowned. As a result, he did not take the oath of fealty along with the rest of the family and the peers of the realm. This may be why, before the outbreak of War, The Duke and Duchess of Windsor felt it right to pay their respects to Adolf Hitler. Instead of staying as state guests, they lodged at 'The Eagles' Retreat', Hitler's own house.

It was here that Hitler first laid the seeds for a plot that was later to prove his undoing. He greeted the Duke and Duchess as if they were King and Queen of England and suggested that they should be so. This was in such contrast to the way he had been treated so far that the Duke felt very pleased. His wounded pride began to swell. The sympathy between the two men developed into a kind of amity, and it didn't take long for them to reach an 'understanding'.

All this, and the story which follows, was told to me by my father. He had three primary sources:-

1. *Ian Fleming*, with whom he worked before, during and after the affair,

2. the *two German officers* whom he met at R.A.F. Tangmere in 1941,

3. *Maxwell Knight*, the Head of the Secret Services.

One point I must stress very strongly. On the direct orders of Winston Churchill, *King George VI was not told nor any other member of the present Royal Family.*

The Royals and the War

Britain warned Germany that if she invaded Poland then a state of war would exist. Hitler had made his plans and Poland was all but massacred in September 1939. Thus, despite all hopes and prayers, World War II began. Under the circumstances, it was not thought appropriate to let the Duke of Windsor serve any role.

But other members of the Royal Family did. The King's other two brothers, the Dukes of Gloucester and Kent, went into active service. His mother, Queen Mary, helped to roll bandages and pack up hospital dressings. The Heir Presumptive, the Princess Elizabeth, worked as a Land Girl[3] and then as a driver in the A.T.S.[4]

This rebuff made the Duke of Windsor almost as furious as the abdication had. He was also seething with rage that the King refused to grant the Duchess of Windsor the style and title of '*Her Royal Highness*'. There was a great conflict of emotions in the Duke's heart. He began to regret his abdication, and even blamed his brother, quite wrongly, for having brought it about.

The Duke of Kent, like other Royals before him, was a member of the Freemasons. Indeed, he was the official Grand Master, but this by no means gave him the power that he imagined. As it happened, the former husband of the Duchess of Windsor had also been a Freemason. During the time of the Royal love affair, he had happily gone along with the public farce so that the true facts might be safely veiled. It is not quite as strange as it sounds then, that a certain masonic clique chose to use the vexed Duke in order to *influence* Hitler's inner councils. One has to recall that *many secret societies had twins in Germany*. The chosen few could exploit these ties for their own benefit.

Not to make too long a story of it, they developed a plot whereby Hitler and England would make a peace treaty. Under its terms, King George VI would be packed off to Canada to act as Governor General. At the same time, the Duke of Windsor would be crowned King of England with the Duchess accepted as Queen.

Such a bold gambit needed the help of people in high places and strong support from key military figures. For this reason, the

3. These were volunteers who worked on farms to replace men who had been conscripted.
4. The Auxiliary Territorial Service, or the women's branch of the army.

proposed treaty would have a special annexe by which *The Act of Union* between England and Scotland would be abrogated, and the United Kingdom dissolved. In its place, Scotland would obtain total independence, even to the extent of having its own, dyed in the wool Scottish King. It went without saying that the two monarchs (of England and Scotland) would rule under Hitler's aegis, very much like the Vichy government of France.

In fact, this so-called peace treaty was little more than an act of surrender. But it would bring two strategic benefits to the Germans:-

1. Firstly it would deny the United States any foothold in Europe.

2. Secondly, given the conquest of Russia, Hitler would be able to launch an attack on the U.S.A. via the Arctic and Alaska which, ironically enough, the Russians had sold to America in 1867.

The plan of campaign was for an invasion to be launched from four quarters at the same time. The first would come from the North, via Russia and Alaska. The second would come from friendly Latin American states. The third would be made from Britain. The fourth would be led by the Japanese forces from the Pacific isles.

I am quite untrained in the field of War Tactics. I cannot help but wonder if Hitler had enough troops to bring off this grandiose plan? Perhaps he was relying on a broken Russian army to join him. Or possibly he felt that Spain and Portugal could be involved. It might even have been that he believed in the occult destiny that his cronies promised him. It did take on the appearance of a battle between good and evil.

Myself, I am just unable to conceive affairs on such a grand scale. But no doubt the Vatican can, and could. The church's help would be crucial with the French part of Canada, and the dictators of South American states. The church was approached. Someone in the church leaked the news to Britain, via the Rumanian Embassy in Lisbon.

How it was Scotched

By sheer good fortune, the section of Military Intelligence that got the news was free of moles and spies. There were fewer fiascos in those days and controls were tighter. Churchill saw at once that they were dealing with dynamite, and it could explode in their faces at any moment. One can see the dilemma:-

1. If the Scots found out about the bit which concerned them, no one could foresee the outcome. The only strong factor was that George VI's Queen was from a noble Scottish family.[5]

2. It was crucial that the English people found out nothing about the link with the reviled Duke of Windsor. If ever it came out, then a surge of sedition could rock the country and threaten army morale.

The War Cabinet was faced with a very grave problem. The plot was not as absurd as it first seemed. They were unanimous in deciding that it could very well work but they were equally fearful of the dangers that might follow its exposure. Heads or tails, we stood to lose a great deal. It was the gravest moment of the war.

A solution was passed up from a certain Commander Ian Fleming who had become obsessed with patriotism. The British would have to mount an offensive that was every bit as cunning as the Hitler plan. They would lure Hitler's deputy, Rudolf Hess, to Britain. It was reckoned, quite rightly as it turned out, that the shock would wreck Hitler's confidence in all his occult advisers. In order to work on Hess, they must feed him 'secret' information from occult sources whom he would be most likely to respect. This was where Aleister Crowley came on to the scene.

One 'secret' that was passed across was the amazing news that he, like Lord Louis Mountbatten, was descended from the ancient family of Hesse and in a favoured occult position. Moreover, the closest living kinsman of Mary Queen of Scots was the Duke of Hamilton.[6] Hess had only to come to Scotland, contact the Duke, and Hess would be acclaimed as rightful King. Then the Scottish people would march against England, at the same time that Hitler would invade from the coast of Europe. Once the Duke of Windsor was back on the throne, English resistance would crumble, and peace would be made with Scotland.

This brew of lies, half lies, and occult jabber did the trick. The message was drummed home to Hess that he would render an

5. Before her marriage to the Duke of York, she had been Lady Elizabeth Bowes-Lyon the daughter of the Earl of Glamis.
6. The Duke's permission had been sought and readily given.

immense service to his Fuhrer. It would be like the love sacrifice of the Teutonic Hero, Siegfried. The world would hail him as the Aryan Messiah.

Nobody was told about the Windsor Plot. The Russians knew nothing about Hitler's plan for an Arctic bridge to America. Not even the Americans were let in on it. Because of his utter loyalty, Churchill made up his mind that the integrity of the Crown must be protected above all else. For this reason the 'Windsor aspect' would be concealed. The Duke of Hamilton agreed. In fact, he made it a condition of lending his name to the strategy that the King would not be harmed in any way.

With delicacy and a deft touch, the Masons did not notice that they were being promoted to higher roles - out of the sphere of concern. As history shows, The Duke of Kent, the Grand Master of Freemasonry, was killed in a strange accident in the year 1942. Thus, when Hess landed in Scotland in a light airplane, his first words were to ask for the Duke of Hamilton. The 'information' had reached its target.

One can almost feel pity for the pathetic, confused wretch as it slowly dawned on him that he had been duped. Not only had he betrayed his own side but he had delivered a great punch below the belt to his beloved Fuhrer. When the full impact struck him, I think it unhinged his mind.

Residual Proofs

Hitler went quite berserk after Hess' defection. This has long been known. He rampaged through the High Command purging the entire system of all psychics, star gazers and occult weirdos. He sent out orders to all field generals to do the same as regards the staff under their control. The Fuhrer no longer trusted any mystic advice - not even his own! It is said that he was a natural psychic and, until that moment, he never made one false move. But now the tide turned and he hardly ever made a good decision again.

I realize that none of this seems feasible today. But none of it was ever mentioned, and we can see why. To reach a fair judgement, you must take several things into account:-

- *the personality of Rudolf Hess, a convinced Occultist*
- *the prestige gained from the Duke of Windsor being part*

- the brilliant revelation that he came from a royal dynasty
- the fact that this might win the war for Germany
- the fact that Aleister Crowley was summoning him
- the fact that he would be King of Scotland
- the fact that he had an heroic destiny.

I have been in contact with other authors, some of them doing research on books which will overlap parts of mine. I am very glad that they have been able to back my own sources.

I am not the only person to know the true facts. There are the Freemasons themselves, to start with. Then there are any surviving members of that old Security Committee. Lastly, we must not forget the chaps who keep the archives - in the Vatican or in Whitehall. But the strangest thing of all is that certain records do still exist. Somebody forgot to destroy them.

Should anyone wish to deny this account, they have to explain some strange facts.

1. all defence outposts in Scotland were given twenty-four hours notice. They were *not to fire* their ack-ack guns at a small airplane coming from Europe.

2. R.A.F. squadrons at Dyce, Leuchars and elsewhere were given orders *not* to attack the airplane but rather to escort it in.

3. When it landed, a lot of people were waiting. When Hess stepped to the ground, he mistook them for a committee of welcome, and *asked at once* for the Duke of Hamilton.

One last word for the Freemasons. You worm into other groups, so others insinuate yours. A branch of the secret service have records of all your dealings, and since 1906 some of your top members have been birds in borrowed plumage. How else did Churchill get to know so much? Not by using a crystal ball in the upstairs, back room of a public house, not far from Scotland Yard.

One man in the know was Commander Ian Fleming. One man not in the know was Wing Commander Dennis Wheatley. When Wheatley got a whiff of these events from elsewhere, he felt very insulted and turned against my father out of injured pride. I don't know if Wheatley was a Mason, but by keeping him out of the operation, they impugned his honour. As far as I know, Wheatley was utterly loyal ... *except to his old friend*, AC.

Mirabila Dictu

I am not expecting the Masonic 'Man of the Year' award. I doubt if the Pope will send me a 'Golden Rose'. And I don't imagine the O.T.O. will ask for a signed photograph. Being a realist, I accept my position, and I defend it.

I even take steps to guard myself against 'former friends'. When someone breaks with me, I lodge their name and a token[7] with magic guardians. If they never hurt me, they are not hurt either. But it works the other way too. If they do me ill, then ill will almost certainly befall them. I trust that everyone will accept that the situation is fair and equitable.[8] The Law says that *nobody may abuse a trust* - even if it was given a long time ago.

My enemies see me either as a bloody nuisance or as someone who can do them harm. Well, I'm not so proud as to think I can't be beaten. But as Cassius Clay might have said, "I dance like a butterfly but I sting like a bee". Most of them try it on furtively, and even then they have found me *too much*.

It is only fair to let everyone know that I have lodged documents where they will do most good. I have also prepared a pamphlet which would tell simple Masons why certain books were banned. By the time this pamphlet has been banned too, it will have appeared as a page in 'The Financial Times' and several other journals.

If I should suddenly be ill, or if I die before a certain date[9], thick envelopes will drop onto many desks. So you must grind your teeth and fight fairly. Aleister Crowley taught me how to set the clock back to 1700! He told me to pass on this piece of advice: *mount watch at the fifth door and do nothing!*[10]

---

7. e.g., their handwriting, a photograph or an old sock!
8. The relationship was first set up on the clear understanding that, if ever it were broken, neither party would seek to harm the other party.
9. As many Freemasons think that poor old Stephen Knight did.
10. Lest they think that these are empty threats: I know about a recent meeting in one of the smaller European countries where they discussed the manning of a certain council. I know about their small delegation that went North on a re-named airline. I know about their party held under a crescent moon. I know about the constellation and the eclipse! If they want me to be more precise, it can be arranged.

17

ONURIS

A hunter whose wife was the vengeful eye of the sun

The Will
I would like to begin this chapter by offering you a short medley of sayings on the subject of will:-

Crowley, Aleister: "Do what thou wilt is the whole of the law. But love is the law - love under (the control of) the will".[1]

Crowley, Amado: "The will is that which reacts against the robot in the mind which gives routine faith to feeling. It is will, and only will, that makes us different from every other creature. It summons us from the mud and steers us towards the stars".[2]

Descartes: "I think and therefore I am".[3] [either 1: because I think, I exist, or 2: by thinking I actually start to be.]

Epictetus: "The good or ill of man lies within his own will".[4]

Franklin, Benjamin: "A fat kitchen, a lean will".[5]

Jesus: ..."Thy will be done on earth as it is in heaven".[6]

Johnson, Samuel: "We know our will is free; and there's an end on't!"[7]

Juvenal: "I wish it. I command it. Let my will take the place of reason".[8]

Lerner, Max: "Man's will creates the things that paralyse his brain and brutalize his heart".[9]

Propertius: "... in great endeavours, even to have had the will is enough".[10]

West, Mae: "If you will keep a diary, make sure it's one that will keep you comfortable in your old age".

1. The Book of the Law, 1904.
2. Tides & Times, 1986.
3. Le Discours et la Méthode.
4. Discourses, I.25 tr. T.W.Higginson.
5. Poor Richard's Almanack.
6. St Matthew, 9.
7. Life of Johnson, 16th October, 1769.
8. Satires 6.223.
9. Actions and Passions, 1949.
10. Elegies, II.x.5.

While staying in Paris in 1919 and early 1920, it is said that Crowley resorted to reading the Tarot cards. He needed a pointer to show him the next step.

He was lodging in a squalid room, next to the Hotel Sphinx, in the quarter off St Michel. Whoever advised him, he found a much sunnier place in the town of Fontainebleau, which was twenty miles south of Paris. Here he settled Leah Hirsig, with her own child. She gave birth to a daughter by Crowley, whom he named Poupée or Dolly.

From Paris, he then fetched a second young woman and child. This was Ninette Shumway who, in return for her keep, was to act as goatherd for the growing flock of kids. As for Crowley, he was kept very busy doing a small favour for a friend. A fellow magician, of the name Gurdjieff, had just fled Russia and was biding his time in Istanbul.[11] Because he wandered about for most of his life, Aleister had a keen nose as an Estate Agent. He found a house, The Chateau de Prieure, some way beyond the town. Gurdjieff and his band moved there in 1922.

Life was not very festive. But Crowley went to Paris each week, and came back with money in his pockets. Among those he met, there was plainly someone, or an institute, who was willing to keep his head above water. At any rate, for a man with nothing, he now managed to support three adults and three children.

Further still, before starting out on the next stage of his mission, Crowley bought First Class tickets to England for Leah and her two infants. These were not the actions of a man who hadn't so much as two pennies to rub together. Yet many of the authors suppose that he and Ninette now headed South, toward Marseilles, for no other reason than pure whim.

After they arrived at the great port, they then veered East and headed toward Italy, roaming along the Cote d'Azur. Some writers insist that he was guided merely by the I-Ching. This seems quite unlikely, unless the I-Ching was also settling all the bills, booking hotels, and sorting out hotel rooms. If this were the case, I wish that certain other holiday companies would adopt the I-Ching too.

Crowley went down the west coast of Italy to Naples. From

11. The city was called Constantinople until the expansion of the Ottoman Empire. It became Constantinople once more in the year 1923.

there he made a bee-line to a small town in northern Sicily, called Cefalu. There he revealed that he had come to found his own Abbey of Thelema!

The Abbey of Thelema

A large sum of cash now lay in his attache case. Some folk insist that this still came from the same, faithful I-Ching. Others now suppose it was a legacy from an aunt. Did the dead aunt think to send it by air-mail? Or do we have to imagine the I-Ching breaking the bank at Monte Carlo? Oh, do come on! This is asking everyone to be a shade too naive! To put it as plainly as possible, one part of the money was payment due for services that had already been rendered. The other part was a capital sum donated by the French Government to set up the Abbey.

At this point in the tale, most writers make a massive leap, plunging straight into the juicy scandals that were said to have happened later. I am going to present the whole story. This will show why the vital points were omitted. What occurred before they got to the abbey is important in spelling out what took place after.

As for the so-called scandal: it was less lurid than has been made out. The known facts as I recount them here, fit as tightly as a jigsaw. You will see quite easily that the entire story was a planned scenario. Oh yes indeed, there was a very simple reason why Crowley went straight to Cefalu. That was the site the French government had chosen. He had a plausible reason for being there. But to make sure he stayed, they accorded him all possible aid - short of cash.

The first night in Cefalu, they used the foulest hotel that he had ever endured in the farthest corners of the world. He was quite an expert on the worst lodgings and most sordid camping sites. Even so, this one broke his nerve. He told them bluntly that he wouldn't be spending a second night there, and made a very quick telephone call. The telling events which now follow are passed over brusquely in most other books.

Chirpily, they agree that an unknown local chanced on their inn, and was keen to rent his dwelling to them. The place was grandly named 'The Villa Barbara', and it lay up in the hills. But it was not a local man at all. It was a quiet Italian who came with a lease. Isn't it odd that no one has ever noticed how promptly this chap appeared on the scene? He pops up pat, dead on cue, as if waiting to make his entrance. But how could he have known? Their voyage had been long, remember, and with transport as it was, who could have guessed how swiftly they would get there? One might almost guess that he had been advised.

Quite amazing, don't you think: within eighteen hours of landing they were dusting out the abbey!

Daily Life

At first glance, it looked less like a spiritual retreat than a derelict farm with no lighting, no drainage and no running water. There was a blatant hole in the parched earth, quite close to the house. One had no need of a telescope to discern that this was the toilet. Although rustic, quaint and charming, one was loth to use it in daylight, but very nervous to go trotting about after dark.

Apart from all else, one had heard tell of poisonous snakes. "If anyone gets bitten," said Crowley, "do not rely on me to suck the venom out!"

Each chose a new spot and marked it with flag, like a golf-links. Aleister picked a place with a fine view and two boulders to hang on to. The funny thing is: none of it shocked them. Even to this very day, every tourist who goes there has qualms about Italian drinking water. As for their plumbing, we all know that this is why the Emperor slid across to Byzantium.

But my father was over the moon with joy. He said the water from a nearby brook was the nearest thing to Malvern springs in taste. I would not be surprised if someone had not put it through some laboratory tests well in advance.

"And just look at the view," he exalted, "One can see all the way to Palermo." And so you could, on a clear day. "This is better than the cliffs of Dover."

On a high rocky outcrop, not very far from the abbey, there were the remains of temples to Jupiter and Diana. He could not have cared less. This kind of classic relic did not interest him. However, he was aware of a former Templar citadel a few hours' drive away. The first thing he did was to set about blessing the place. He made the great central room act as their temple, and covered the walls with drawings. Some of them, he later reported, were "amiably obscene".

I don't think that my father's virility was ever affected by either extremes of temperature. From the snowy peaks of China to African deserts as hot as ovens, his sex drive seems never to have been weakened. Life in a city tended to drain his energy, so he had no intention of acting like a prude while romping in the remote hills of Sicily.

"It was quite normal to trot about in the nude," he told me. "On some moments we wore even less!" I must leave you to reflect on what that might mean.

One of the scenes that he painted was of a man being buggered by the God, Pan. Anyone who writes about the abbey seems to be very wrapped up in this. Either they are very keen to show that Crowley was totally depraved, or else that picture excites them more than it should. In either case, it was not done in order to cause outrage to anyone since it was not intended to be seen.

"If Pan is still lurking, it's more likely to be here than Chipping Sodbury[12], so it's as well to know what 'tootling his pipe' actually means!"

Pan was the God of Nature, and was usually represented as half goat and half man. This was meant to express the sheer power and urgency of his great task as guardian of the wild i.e, of plants and animals. Let me put it this way, Pan was neither pansy nor wilting violet! He could drive men mad. He could instil them with blind frenzy. Most important, he could fill them with dreadful fear that would make them drop all 'superior will' in order to survive. He was the icon or the god essence of man. He did not just represent the aspect of man which derived from nature. He was that which made man different from other animals.

Whatever else he might be doing here, Crowley also planned to get back to basics and to teach his friends the path that led to knowing the self.

Persona Non Grata

Oddly - his removal was ordered from Italy by Mussolini himself. They left for Tunisia on 1st May, 1923, followed by agents who kept carefully in the shade. The crucial points to notice here are that Tunisia is closer to Sicily than Corsica is to mainland France.

---

12. This is a small market town in Oxfordshire. I suspect that his tongue fell on this because the syllable 'Sod' suited his purposes.

The superb vista over the Bay of Palermo also gave AC a nice view of Italian Navy movements. What you may not remember is that Italy had conquered Libya in 1911/12, whereas Tunisia, next door, had been under French Protection since 1881.

One can see the French concern, knowing that Italy was looking at the whole of the Mahgreb[13] with a hungry eye. In the early 1930s she invaded Ethiopia. All her naval traffic would have been seen by other Adriatic states who kept a very sharp look-out. Easier and less obvious, if ships passed down the east coast, using the Tyrrhenian Sea, and slid through the Straits of Messina.

He had been in Sicily for just over three years. Most authors accept at face value what Crowley wrote about his own life. When it suits their purpose, they scoff at what he says and warn us that everything should be taken with a pinch of salt. But as regards the Cefalu affair, Colin Wilson[14] for one swallows it hook, line and sinker, even where it is hearsay.[15] In so doing, of course, he has fallen for the very hoax that Crowley, and the French Secret Service, had so nicely prepared.

- Crowley went to Russia more than once, but the first visit was to scout out the chance of working for the Foreign Office. On these visits he met Rasputin and Gurdjieff.

- Gurdjieff, the Russian - nay, we must be correct and call him the Georgian[16] mystic - had a centre of studies in the same town as AC's rented house.[17] It was Crowley who found it for him after he fled from his own land.

- Crowley was very familiar with North Africa. He had often been to Egypt, and had made visits to Morocco and Tunisia. His trips into Libya had been errors since he was never certain just how far 'Aiwass' steered him, when they went looking for The Book of Desolation.

- Crowley was highly adept in Arabian magic and had studied

---

13. This is an Arabic word, meaning sunset and it used to describe the Arab countries of North Africa, as opposed to Syria, Jordan etc.
14. Colin Wilson, 'Aleister Crowley, The Nature of the Beast', Aquarian Press, 1987.
15. Early in the Chapter 7, p117, Wilson writes: "According to Frank Harris (quoted by Symonds) Crowley left behind him in New York a string of dud cheques. He was hoping that the OTO would have money in the kitty, but soon discovered that the treasurer had embezzled it." There is no support for the truth of this statement, except for the fact that the Treasurer of the OTO had nicked the funds! Why would one mention any of this unless one is using all the puff one can get to blow a great raspberry?
16. Just like Josef Stalin (real name Josef Vassarionovitch Dzhugashvili 1879 to 1953) who, as a student in a seminary, had lodged with the Gurdjieff family.
17. i.e, Fontainebleau.

the work (found in Paris) of 'Abra-Melin, the Sage'.

- Crowley did once write some false support for a German paper that was printed in the USA.

- He was known to and was on friendly terms with many members of the British Intelligence system.

- He went to Paris on a magical retreat, after Leah aborted.

- He went again in January 1922, and was taken into custody near Boulogne after being 'mistaken' for a someone else. This arrest was a thin disguise. The French had urgent need to meet him and find out how much the Italians had rumbled.

- He went to Tunisia again to meet Jane Wolfe.

- He was arrested again on being expelled from France in March 1929. Yet one month later, he was on board a ferry and went openly in and out of Boulogne with no questions asked. His object, by the way, was to meet with my mother. I was born nine months later, in January 1930!

- France had vast colonial domains inside the land mass of Africa as well as on the northern coast.

How are we to read all this? Was it all no more than pure chance? I am telling you that there was a joint plan, signed and approved by more than one country. Crowley was acting as an agent, and his cover was perfect:

1. he was a Magician, and this was all it took to make most Italians avert their gaze. Wherever he went, there was the sound of people spitting over their crossed fingers to guard against the devil.

2. he was eccentric which, in Italy, is roughly equal to being wrong in the head.

3. he was English, and that was enough in itself. When you look for a spy, you expect him to be well hidden. It took a long time for them to realize what Crowley was up to.

On first hearing, this story may sound far too absurd. Yes, well, there'd be no damn point in making it obvious, would there? This is precisely why it worked! What I say is the truth. Either we accept it or else ... all the other things become pure idiocy. And as I have already pointed out: Crowley was not a fool.

18

NAB-TA-DJESER

Anubis as Lord of the sacred land

Metapolitics[1]

It ought to be obvious by now that there was, and still is, an occult society tucked away in a corner of northern France. It covers the area from Boulogne to Ostend and to Lille. The members were a very mixed group, with workers, managers and one or two people who held high office in local or regional affairs. There was at least one banker, and someone who held a key post in a very large industry.

All in all, this group could have a crucial 'push' on the forward planning in this part of France. If the Prefect of the day was not 'in' on it himself, then you can be sure that he was kept closely informed. He would also be pliant and open to influence. Bear in mind how often my father had been chucked out of France, and declared 'persona non grata'. Yet no one seem too worried by his habit of coming back in!

Just think of all the agents who 'knew about' Crowley. Not just local police, but the gendarmes, secret police, frontier police and the chaps who worked for the Customs. Are we to suppose that not one of these men noticed when Crowley came and went as it pleased him? Or had they all been told to turn a blind eye, as a matter of policy? At two o'clock in the morning, when I have passed through one of the ports, the officials seem too weary to inspect any cars. But they are not as lax as they seem. They have got back-ups on the boats who tell them which cars to examine!

In the 1920s they were all acting under orders from the Quai d'Orsay[2], and various members of the government! The Interior

---

1. The study of influences "behind" political events, i.e. the grander view of things.
2. Rather like "Downing Street", this street name usually means: the French Foreign Ministry, and all that this entails.

Minister, the Foreign Minister, the Prime Minister and the President - at least these four had to know about, and agree to the facts. Between them and the lowly clerks at the ports, there must have been almost a hundred civil servants who were in on the intrigue. As I said before, Masonry is rife in the French system so are we to assume that they too were helping Crowley along? Or to be frank, did Aleister know that the men he was working for were personal foes? Was he just faking it?

The answer, of course, is no! He knew quite well what he was doing. He went along with the farce of being banished from France. He knew quite well for whose benefit the show was mounted, and whom the government wished to fool. It is a simple fact that Crowley was quite happy to fool them too. I will go further and suggest that the whole exploit might have been his idea from the start. He could have sold the package to France as a way of keeping her hands clean.

But at the very same time though, no one's hands looked cleaner than those of Crowley himself. Now whom did he wish to dupe? Could it have been Soviet Russia, who was then in the process of expanding? Was it the new Germany who was rallying fast from defeat in the Great War? Was it the Masons, who handled most events that occurred in Europe? Or, more dreadful still, was it his French "friends" whom he hoped to cheat?

Let me give you just one more tit-bit to chew over. There were certain forces within France which he thought it right to betray. What forces were these? Well, when Nazi Germany did invade France, there was an existing body of people who were eager to please Hitler. They formed a puppet government at the small town of Vichy. They handled the rest of France on lines decided in Paris. They did not hesitate to expose the Jews and assist in their mass transfer to the death camps. They did their best to gain the confidence of the Resistance and then gave their names to the Gestapo. Aleister knew that this face of France existed already but that it was very darkly veiled.

The people involved were not trying to betray their country so much as make it glorious again. They were all members of a certain cult whose roots can be traced back to well before the Cathars. They say nought and reveal nought. They leave us to speculate and allow us to speak or write about our silly guesses or opinions. They let out hints about their dignity and status. They neither confirm, nor deny, that there are high churchmen in their ranks. There is a silent smile on their lips as whispers are heard about possible links with royalty. My father knew them for what they really were: *devotees of black magic*! They were, they are, and they always have been ready to sacrifice millions of lives to venerate their god of darkness.

"Do you know his name?" asked Crowley, when he explained all this to me. "*The Seigneur du Mal, or Lord of Evil*, is one of his titles. *Le Roi d'Enfer*, or King of Hell, is another."

Ladies and Gentlemen, my news is not very pleasant but I'm afraid *there are people in France who worship the Devil*.

The Missing Link
The crux of this whole affair is the first OTO in Germany. Crowley found out how firmly the Golden Dawn and OTO were based on a kind of tyranny. It was all hushed up, of course. Or else it was put forward as quite a different story. The tale about the bitter strife between the two key names - Samuel Lidell Mathers and Aleister Crowley is a brewed-up blend of blather.

Crowley was quite content to go along with this deception and let it go the rounds. He even added one or two extra touches of his own to lend it colour and make it sound more credible. He wanted that 'secret group' inside Germany, as well as its offshoots in other parts of Europe, to regard him as an egotist, pure and simple. It was crucial that none of them should get wind of danger or suspect him of elaborate duplicity. In fact, it became only too clear what was afoot when the Italian and German Axis was forged in 1939, and later widened to take in Japan.

In this respect there are some very interesting dates that are worth studying. Josef Stalin came to power in Russia in 1922. Adolf Hitler became the head of the NAZI party in 1923. Benito Mussolini came to power in Italy in 1922. Gurdjieff set up his study centre at Fontainebleau in France in the year 1922. *All the while*, Crowley was living in a decrepit farm in Sicily!

This isn't the whole story by a long chalk. Josef Stalin knew Gurdjieff in person. When Stalin was a student priest, he was a paying guest in the Gurdjieff home. At the same time, his friend was visiting some lamas in Tibet.[3] This fact assumes even greater

3. This is not so surprising when one realizes that Gurdjieff was born at Azochozki, east of Lake Baikal, and was of Mongol descent.

significance when you put it side by side with another one: Crowley *met both Gurdjieff and Rasputin at Mount Athos!*

It is widely recognized already that Crowley knew Karl Haushoffer. But that same Karl Haushoffer paid *at least five visits to Gurdjieff* at his study house in Tibet. As if all that were not strange enough, we now add just one ingredient: *Karl Haushoffer taught the young Adolf Hitler about magic.* There you are! The conundrum is all but solved.

It is a bit of a tangled tale, I agree, but the tactics had been under preparation for a very long time indeed. A great deal of what passes for human history is in fact a study of power moves and rivalry. The people behind all this were a lot more patient than you and me and they covered up their tracks quite well. Do you still think that it sounds a little bit too weird? Hold on to your hat, then, because I haven't quite finished the story.

The first Russian troops to break into Berlin in 1945 were in very great haste. The official version is that all the Allies were anxious to establish a foothold in the German capital and so play a dominant role in the future. But the Russian troops made rather a strange find. By accident, or by design, they stumbled on a thousand corpses of Tibetan origin. All of them were wearing German military uniforms, but not one of them bore any insignia nor any mark of rank.[4]

Dear readers, none of this may be welcome news for the bigger ears of the state machine. They will discount it if they are deftly skillful, or else deny it if they are imbeciles. Since they are neither skilled nor stupid, I think they'll resort to all the old insults again. Yet the fact is that my father deserves the highest awards that England or France can bestow.

He did far more than any of you realize to prevent the outbreak of the Second World War. Once it had begun, he then did his best to end it. Of course, these matters are muffled by walls of silence and befogged by the attacks on his name. They do not want you to know the truth about the evil of that war. History alone may one day reveal the extent to which the whole world was hounded by real agents of evil.

---

4. see: (a) Maurice Bess, 'A Pictorial History of Magic and the Supernatural', Spring Books, London; Louis Pauwels, Jacques Bergeier, 'The Dawn of Magic', Panther Books, London; J.H.Brennan, 'The Occult Reich', Futura Publications, 1974.

The Steward

My father had a secret doctrine which he kept very close to his chest. I knew about it. He could not help but tell me. For my own part, I was impressed by the way he valued these precious ideas. He spoke of them in a hushed, husky voice as someone moved by a profound respect.

"She is not dead," he said strangely. "She is not dead but sleeping.[5] We must walk in whispers that she be not awakened before her due time."

It was many years before I realized just how often he was quoting from 'The Book of Desolation'. I have read it too, of course. Like all the Shakespeare one ever studied at school, some of the more beautiful phrases spring unbidden to one's lips in the course of normal conversation. I gave up biting my tongue a long time ago. I cannot stop myself from letting these things escape. If I tried to be more discreet then I would seem as taciturn and secretive as modern oracles whose mouths open only when paid.

One of the events in Crowley's life is not explored as deeply as it should have been. While he was in Mexico in 1900, he deeply impressed a certain Don Jesus Medina. This man was head of another magical order and led Crowley through its thirty-three degrees in a matter of a few weeks. As a result of this experience, Crowley formed his own new order called 'The Lamp of Invisible Light' and made Don Jesus the second member. All this, mind you, some sixty years before Castaneda[6] had his meetings with Don Juan! I wonder if Castaneda thought of asking Don Juan if he belonged to any group of Shamans?

Of course, in my own person I was no more fitting than anybody else to have merited his trust. I make no bones about that. But then I was his son, remember, and like Abraham with his darling Isaac, he dragged me up the sacred mountain to a sanctuary. He was all too heedful of an inner command to keep the truth safe.

That makes us both sound arrogant, I dare say, but one is not free to pretend otherwise. The truth is whatever it is, and one must not feel ashamed to have seen it unveiled. That Aleister was

5. see: St Matthew, 9:24: "The Maid is not dead but sleepeth." This suggests that either Matthew was making an oblique reference to The Book of Desolation, or he was familiar with the teachings which gave rise to it.
6. Carlos Castaneda, 'The Teachings of Don Juan', University of Californian Press 1968.

chosen, in spite of all his flaws, is a sign that should give courage to all. That is how he saw it too. That is what he believed. "Let them paint me as a fool," he said. "As long as they are laughing, they are not seeking!" In part, this explains what the mockery and capering were all about: he was an unworthy vessel that proved the truth. It never ceased to astonish him that he had been chosen.

"It began as a game," he told me. "It began as a bucket of water chucked in my mother's face. But then it became true. Little by little, one syllable at a time, the hate turned into regret and the regret into love." He would sigh so deeply then. "The dung beetle began rolling pearls." He was referring here to the sacred beetle of ancient Egypt which, in rolling dung into small balls and pushing them apparently for miles, was taken to be a holy symbol. The pearl, in AC's language was a symbol of sperm and therefore life.

But he was not the owner of Truth. That which had been given could not be seen as any kind of private property. It was a trust. It was something that had been put into his care and he saw himself as the guardian *pro tempore*. His job was to confide it in those who were capable of accepting it, while keeping it hidden from eyes that were merely curious. He had a duty to protect it from those who would exploit it for ill. For it was not just *knowledge* that he kept in his heart but the violent energy which it carries. He tarried beside a babbling stream, knowing that it married the *Mother of All Waters* round the next turning and went boiling into the abyssal sea.

He saw the defects in his friends and henchmen, and realized that in handing truth across to them he would be failing his duty somehow. They were too mature, too sure of themselves and too much inclined to *this world here and now*. In brief, the mortar had already set in their souls.

What he actually needed was a juvenile heart, a green mind, and a soul with a similar potential to his own. That was why he made me. That is why I was born. There was an aim to all his weary calculus, just as there was purpose behind all the complex strategy. I am not vaunting with pride nor do I announce this merely to strut my style. I stick my neck out because you must know. The Law requires that you be told.

So I am now the Guardian, and I have been so for almost half a century. One might well think otherwise to judge by other folk's reactions. There have been times when I wondered if my forehead were branded or my body bore all the symptoms of leprosy. So far as A C's own friends were concerned, they would rather I did not exist. I represented a problem. So they kept me an outcast from their councils. But it is worth recalling the myth of Oedipus: the King who suffered not for any willful misdeed, but because he was singled out and walked in the company of Gods.

Once again, that sounds like pride. But was Jesus proud of being the Christ? When they accused Him of wanting to be King, did he deny it or agree? The King, you remember, was the chosen offering who died on behalf of the whole tribe. To die and to suffer ... to accept the woes that are due to others ... it is a terrible destiny, hardly bearable. Very few men can face up to it.

But when you do, fewer men still can examine your eye. This is how a man can become the mirror which turns reality round. He sees as if through a prism, and what he sees is a lunatic image of his own iniquity. "What could be worser," asked Aleister once, "than being right, and being thought wrong?"

He knew as well as anyone else that in the English language, worse is already the comparative of bad. According to the rules of grammar, one simply must not say "worser". But Aleister was breaking the rules. He was trying to express the notion that there are degrees inside the concept of "worse", and that none of this is yet the worst thing of all.

He was very fond of Shakespeare, as I have already said. He was very struck by a passage from 'King Lear' (IV.i.27): "The worst is not, So long as we can say, 'This is the worst.'"

19
BAT

She who is in the sistrum, her voice the magic of music

The Treasure

What is it then that the Guardians watch over? What is this treasure that they guard? If I replied to that question in the literal wording with which it is usually asked, I would be out of a job, hapless, and without a pension. I would be on bread and water for evermore and you would all suppose that I wasn't a very efficient Guardian. But luckily, I am no black Othello who worries greatly about his good name, but a white sentinel, faithful to his duty, who watches the stars falling.

But then, although you may be new to this kind of thinking and rather naive about the mystical path, you are not quite children either. How much simpler it would be if you were. Then at least I could credit you gladly with a probity of purpose. You may be ignorant, yes, I will grant you that. But you are not at all as innocent as you like to pretend. Whatever you have done with your life, you did it with will. It was no autumn leaf being swirled by the wind. It was no fallen blossom being dashed by the rain.

Never cry that you were helpless to resist, for the gods have promised that no man shall be tempted farther than his natural will to triumph. Madmen know this. The moon shows it. Logic and reason are flawed engines. No, you are not children to whom father explains the facts of adult life. The knowing is in you and you did not look, because you strayed from the path at the first wild whistle. "Oh Danny boy, the pipes, the pipes are calling ..."

This is not a Jeremiad of rebuke though it may well resemble one in tone. I am showing you why I am forbidden to tell you what you are thirsty to know. You have neither the ears to hear nor the imagination to understand. I must defend you from the aftermath of your own folly in exactly the same way that I do not let infants play with guns. It is not a treasure that I guard so much as your precious souls that I protect. Oh, I could tell you some wonderful tales, and so soothe your outrage. But it is more fitting that I tell you why you are not yet prepared. By carrot or stick, by kiss or a kick, I am obliged to convince you that this instant is eternal.

One halts halfway through a stride, his foot hovering on the abyss, while another is dancing the tango with a rose piercing his mouth. It's as if they conspired to forget that life is a place of waiting. They convert it into a theatre and hope to God that the show is real. But the smiles are fixed, the laughter is brittle, and the flashing lights merely veil the panic. How giddy the young wine in gulping old throats when it helps one swallow one's heart!

"Don't blame me," said Crowley one day. "It is not a game and I am not amusing myself. You have been brought up, most likely, to believe in a pitying God who would incline from eternal glory to launder your raiment and cleanse your eye." He gave a cough, an arumph. "So you believe God is a Teddy Bear with red ribbons and bells on. Or else He is a fat, red, avuncular Santa Claus who gives, gives, gives and never demands payment."

He shook his head. "How cosy! How tender! And how wrong! Look again, my lad, and do not take sentiment for fact nor hope for truth!"

In the three days between December 3rd and 6th, 1909, a strange ceremony took place on Mount Dal'leh Addin, near to the village of Bou-Saada, in Morocco. Crowley, along with Victor Neuberg, a friend he had known at Cambridge, invoked the 'Demon of the Abyss', whose name was Choronzon. Many occult scholars see this as the most amazing act of magic ever attempted during this century, which simply goes to show how gullible they are. Once again, the real details are not quite as tradition would have us believe.

You don't have to believe all the things that Crowley ever said, you know. Neither are you obliged to accept his written works as something akin to holy scripture. As for his diaries - ah well, why should he lie in his diaries? Well I know some diaries, and perhaps you do too, which would make Casanova seem like a gelded peacock, for example! I also know that certain young men

140

who, embroiled in the plots and schemes of love, have left their diary where it could be stumbled on. As for that dear Victor Neuberg, be careful what heed you take of him. He was not exactly his own man, before or after.

Once again, my father has been at it. He knew the Savoy operas quite well. He liked most of them, but was very fond of 'The Mikado'. So when he told me what he had done, he added some "mere corroborative detail",[1] and I knew that I could believe him. I mean to say, if you re-read his own account of this Moroccan interlude, don't you get the whiff of English humour?

Something happened, yes, but the whole event has been dipped in crude clowning - to put certain people off the scent. The only comment I wish to add here is: everyone agrees that Crowley had power over demons. Their names were not those suggested by Eliphas Levi so I'm afraid that Choronzon just isn't in it. We'd be closer if we called them Butcher, Grinder or Eater of Minds.

So when he said: "God is seventy times more dreadful than the Devil", he knew what he was talking about. "God can shatter one's mind," he went on. "The first time I met Him, I confess that I shit my breeches!"

The Fabric of Truth

While I was doing my military service, I started to have sudden attacks of violent pain in my abdomen and I would double-up or drop to the ground. This is not really the sort of thing that Top Brass like to see in the course of a grand parade. It tends to spoil the effect. So they sent me off to the army hospital at Catterick, in Yorkshire. To my great surprise they found that one of my testes had not dropped. It must seem rather strange that I had never noticed this myself.

It is even stranger that the panel of doctors had missed it during my first medical check-up. But there you are, you see. It's just one of those things! It rattles me to talk about my genitals so openly but wait till you see where it's leading. To be fair to the doctors, I must explain that the testicle was more or less descended but the spermatic cord was too short. For reasons unknown, or perhaps cold weather, it would retract from time to

---

1. The character Pooh-Bah, the Lord High Everything Else, never used a short word where a long one would do.

time, and give the sensation of being booted in the crotch!

I was still nineteen, remember, and the hospital was run as much by military rule as by medical code. It was quite an ordeal standing to attention before a panel of doctors, dropping one's trousers, while they poked around like circus moilers trying to mend a trapeze. When they had finished, they asked me if I had any questions. It took a few moments to get my breath back. My most urgent question was if I would have two fine testicles once everything was over.

"Don't worry," yawned one young doctor in weary boredom. "If anything were to go wrong we could always slip in a glass eye!"

I turned my head and stared at him so angrily he went pale. He had a car accident two weeks later and lost his own left eye. I do not suggest that I caused this very grave accident. It was none of my wishing. The only thing that went through my head was how I'd liked to have kicked him in the crotch. As far as I was concerned, it was just another of those strange things that occur from time to time. They grew more and more frequent as I grew older, and the light dawned fully a few months before I became a Master. I did not realize it at the time but the 'spirit keepers' which Aleister Crowley had given me, had followed their instincts and snapped at him.

A truly spooky thing happened when I was put in the surgery ward. In the next bed was a sergeant from the Education Corps whose name was Bernie Tocker. With a name like that, he had become a very patient man. We hit it off well together and began to swap news. The first thing we learned was that we both shared the same birthday. Moreover, the two of us were born at exactly four o'clock in the afternoon, just in time for tea!

"What are you in for?" I asked casually.

He whipped back his blankets to show me his shaven belly. "One ball not dropped," he beamed.

I whipped back my own blankets and we just stared like two men stricken dumb. In both our cases, it was the left one. We were very deeply shaken and talked about it endlessly. He was very clever at numbers and began making frantic notes. I don't know how many babies were born each day in Britain nor how many choose that particular day. A certain number, I don't doubt. But two of us had the same uncommon defect. We go into the same hospital and the same time, and end up in adjacent beds. We are operated on at the same time. What are the odds of all that happening by chance? Bernie worked it out. *"Twenty five million to one,"* was his answer.

Another little thing: his dad had died in 1947. He had been a stage magician.

Figure 2.
LEVELS OF RITUAL

1. Rituals Affecting You

THE GRADIENT	THE PATH	THE SELF
Knowing Self.	Entering craft.	Apprenticeship.
Effacing flaws.	Initiating.	Master's Jubilee.
Acting Faculty.	Three Candles.	Making Twin.
Self-fulfilment.	Meeting Children.	Calendric: Lun/Sol.
Healing.	Wedding.	Interventions.
Blessing.	Suspending.	Divination.
	Quitting.	

2. Rituals Affecting Another

LIFE COURSE	INNER/OUTER EVENTS
Invocation Earth.	Spirit, soul, sickness, wind, hurricane.
Invocation Air.	Project, building, material, earthquake.
Invocation Water.	Mind, opinion, quarrel, madness, tears.
Invocation Fire.	Do/undo, create/destroy, sex/love, war.

3. Rituals Affecting Family or Small Business

ROOT & BRANCH	CLIMATE
Candle Tree: past to future.	Shining mountain.
Origin of life, posterity.	Hagoday, nightmare.
Destiny in the Beyond.	Fears true, legend real.
Burning light of soul.	Passing beyond.
Life-force and posterity.	Locating gateways.
Truth guides wanderers home.	Opening & closing doors.

4. Rituals for Neighbourhood

Extending shield.
Ill-will, malice.
Sacrifice of Pure Love.
Defence of Homes.
Paying for Calamity.

5. Rituals for Community

Blessing land/beasts.
Blessing work/tools.
Blessing People.
Banishing Whirlpools.
Banishing foci of evil.

6. Rituals for World

Sickness rides the wind.
Hatred behind wars.
Monsters in bottles.
Hammering the sea.
Drumming the land.
Killing the fire.

7. Rituals for the Beyond

Releasing earth-bound anguish.
Banishing opportunist visitors.
Seeking advice.
Asking for exemptions.
Invoking the dead.
Calling a God.

It is at moments like these, that the great weaving machine seems to stop. You can see the weft and warp as separate strands for an instant. You catch a glimpse of something that moves on the other side of the loom. You believe, you think, you hope that you see the fingers that fling the shuttle.

Embarking on Magic

When the occult confronts them in a serious way, most people will go on arguing about whether or not it exists. They say that many of its tenets are so difficult and many of its beliefs have no grounds. They consider it most unlikely that they would ever accept it. Unlike other puddings, they judge this one without a single nibble.

The fact is they are scared. In spite of exams passed and books read, this is one area on which they have studied no syllabus. The nearest they ever got has been 'folklore' and 'The Story of Robin Hood'. The band of merry men got disbanded, you remember; too highly strung and feathers kept dropping off their arrows! But so far as the average man in the street is concerned, there are certain details it is prudent not to know. Despite that, he will queue to see films that scare him shitless, if you'll pardon the expression.

I'm afraid that the great majority of so-called psychics are in much the same boat, if you see what I mean. A few crystals, a bit of New Age music, and a pack of dainty tarot cards ... and there you are: in harmony with the 'all'. That too is what we might call deceiving the soul. Like tourists in Carnaby Street in giddy mood, they buy the daftest clothes just because they're led by fancy, not by truth. I may go against the tide, but occultism and magic are not open to democratic vote.

Fashions change, last year's music is out, while fatigued faces parade for their turn to enjoy 'instant success' and fame. Don't seek the Holy Grail in a dusty amusement arcade. Don't let your mind be heavily altered by the lyrics of a song. The truth is absolute and your only choice is to dismiss it or accept.

Like timid youths, too shy to embrace a girl, people realize that music was playing only when it stops! "I do not run after students, like a milliner slapping hats on their head!" said Aleister Crowley. "It doesn't matter whether they like me because it is not myself that's on offer! Damn silly arses! They will never realize how close they came to ecstasy!"

There were two things Crowley blamed for this muddled approach to religion. Firstly, people expect God to be twin to Father Christmas, that is to say: roundish, genial and ever ready to let you sit on his knee and bend His ear. He is the epitome of justice and mercy, and quite fond of pushing rich young men through the eye of a needle. Secondly, it doesn't much matter what we believe so long as we are 'nice' to each other. That is where Attila the Hun, Genghis Khan and Hitler all went wrong ... they did things nastily.

In other words, even though we don't believe in God, we know what sort of God we'd want. We have a list of criteria and, if not a photo, then a police drawing in mind. He doesn't exist, of course, but if He did, this is what he'd be like. It is pure fantasy, of course. It is a collage built up of our own sighs and sorrows. He'd have sweets in his pockets like grandad, and he'd bang the bullies' heads together at the school gates. He'd find a home for all the kittens so none would have to be drowned, and dad's business would prosper. That is what Jehovah means, doesn't it? Or so we like to think.

"The first thing a newcomer must do," said Crowley, "is to unknow everything that has been put in his head. Let him stay out of the sanctuary and start work in the attic." He laughed hugely and slapped his thighs, a Father Christmas gesture now that I think of it!

Here he was alluding to the human body as both a house and a temple. In this allegory, the head becomes a dusty old library or an attic where unwanted rubbish is hidden out of sight. If I asked him where the temple was or the inner sanctum, he would say "In the tripes!" Even then it was half joke and half truth - half shock and half puzzle. He was telling me once again that my concept of the innards (bowels, faeces and so on) blinded me to a vital point: that the ethereal body was quite probably a mirror reversal.

Then, all of a sudden, he seemed to fall into a state of brooding sadness.

"I knew some people whose special pastime was to learn verses from the bible. Can you imagine, they would sit down each night and memorize a dozen or so. Every Sunday, they would meet at one another's house in turn, and hold a competition." He gnawed his bottom lip as if in pity.

146

"There would be district finals," he said in a choking voice. "This was followed by county finals, and then, as a grand finale, they would compete for the national title." He began to sputter now, and I realized he was laughing.

"The generous prize, after all that effort, was another copy of the Bible!" He held his hands to his face, a serviette spread between them, and chortled like a child.

"My friends lost," he howled, stamping his feet on the floor. "They could not give the source for Mary had a little lamb!" He was in such a state of glee, he almost couldn't speak. If anybody could be said to have rolled about in hilarity, it was Aleister, right there and then.

"It isn't from the bible," I remarked in all innocence. "It's part of a nursery rhyme."

"Exactly!" he shouted. "But they didn't know that. They had only learned the Bible."

His laughter was so immense, I was even infected by it, but I must confess, I didn't get the joke. I worried about it for quite a few years and it dawned on me very gradually. He calmed down slowly. You know how it is - like a volcano that rumbles into uneasy silence.

"Oh yes," he said, a faint twinkle in his voice. "Begin with dust and cobwebs. They wouldn't know a diamond if they saw one. Not yet at any rate!"

Illiterati

I know now what he was getting at. He was not just thinking of pious people who are blind to reality. He was talking about everyone, occult students too, who are so smug that it never once crosses their minds to wonder if they haven't assumed things wrongly. He was talking about people who have no grounds at all for thinking as they do - no grounds other than a private, inner creed.

Man's emotions are no doubt more refined and subtle than those of animals. We have all seen a dog explode with fury. They thresh around in parked cars showing you what they'll do if you attempt to get in. You haven't the slightest intention of going in, but in case you change your mind, it is telling you that it's prepared to die. But does it cower in disgrace when it realizes it has been defending the wrong car? Does it lick the hand it fed on

147

after chasing a postman from the wrong garden? No. Dogs are protected from such fatal shame. They never believe that their cause was wrong. That is why dogs don't stop. They just go on. It is asking too much to expect them to apologize.

Well human emotions may be more refined, but in some situations they are almost identical. Being as stubborn as a donkey is just one example. Once a man sinks his mental teeth into something, he's not going to let go even if it drags him towards a certain death. Another one is what Edward de Bono calls 'lateral thinking'. A man can, and will, make huge leaps of logic, leaving out all the middle steps, and just 'intuit' a solution. I think Indiana Jones probably belongs in this category, along with James Bond. You know the process. You take Fact A. You then submit it to a procedure B. You believe in what you've done and it has always worked. So you'll gamble your soul on the outcome being C. Tough luck when it's M or Z!

In the esoteric field, or in the spiritual park - one meets droves of people like this. Many of them are elated to meet the son of the famous Aleister Crowley. They ask me what colour I prefer, whether I eat meat, and do I sleep in a Japanese bed. I say I'm not finicky whose bed I sleep in, and they smile politely. They then proceed to lull my dubiety, soothe my ego, and diagnose where I have gone wrong. Quite often, I am invited to speak at this or that meeting, only to find that most of the audience prefer to argue and would much rather trap me. (They have never succeeded!)

Now where does this inflated degree of pride come from? In some cases it is a morbid symptom of something seriously wrong in their heads. I have called it "the Billy the Kid" syndrome. Each one has a desperate desire to prove that he is the fastest gun in the west - or in my case, the magician who knows most. The easiest way out would be to change them into frogs. One must first make sure where the good ship Rainbow Warrior might be. Nor should one forget that there are magic mirrors.

148

20

MAGA

The crocodile, son of Seth, dangerous to life

The Church and Evil

Crowley told me that although other religious sects were fresher
on the scene, the church carried on curing devilry by such trusty
methods as extreme torture and cruel death. The odd burning
was good for filling up the churches and imbued a deeper piety in
the soul. It raised morale by showing good people that bad
people got what they deserved.

Even the poor felt clean and more virtuous - even though the
smell of roasting meat was tempting. One simply made sure that
the ashes were well raked over to prevent any so-called friends
from snatching relics. "Relics, my arse!" barked Crowley. "The
starving crowd would scoff the gobbets it found among the
cinders."

None of this means that the Devil had actually gone. Perhaps
he just got fed-up of that gaudy red suit. Perhaps he felt too
flashy with horns and a tail. Or perhaps long forks were just too
clumsy on buses. If he is still in residence then he'll be strutting
around town in an expensive outfit designed by Yves St Laurent.
That's my guess, for what it's worth. He would prefer Jean-Paul
Gaultier but for two small facts. First, he hates 'La Traviata', and
thinks that Jean-Paul wrote it.[1] Second, he can't bear his link with
Madonna which is quite logical, when you think about it.

Apart from this, today's devil is really with it. He is cool - on
the outside at least. At the average rock concert it's hard to tell if
he's with the nutters on stage or the maniacs in the audience. I
slip this in here and now because today's pop scene is *the devil's
happy hunting ground.* We do all realize, I trust, that many of the
major stars have been trapped by drugs and tricked by black

1. The love-story on which Verdi's opera is based, was written by Theophile Gauthier.

magic[2]. Mark well my words! Too many of them overdose, have crashes, get drowned, get shot, or decline in clinics where cells are padded in purple silk.

Those words, *purple silk*, remind me where we are heading. By design or accident, that growth of evil could be the Pope's doing. The Vatican has the largest spy network in the world, with Israel coming a close second. When money was needed to help defeat Communism and free Central Europe, then of course the church could find the funds. That was God's work, you see. That was money well spent.

But how unlucky it is that Peter never has quite enough pence to relieve the poverty of Latin America or help stave off disease. Not only has the Church been silent on the subject of fascist despots, but she also clamped down on any priest who defended the new 'liberation theology'.

Well, I am delighted that Poland is free. The poor of that country can now give freely to the church once more whereas, before, the state just took it from them. They still suffer of course. There are still so many burdens. The price of bread is still high. The cost of holidays in France are still beyond the pocket. I expect things will seem so much rosier, as soon as the Vatican has moved to Warsaw. Oh, no one can possibly doubt that the Pope has had a lot to do with the counter revolution that took place. Neither can one deny that Jean-Paul II has a special way with words!

Sometimes, though he seems to go a step too far. To put it simply, His Holiness can put his foot in his mouth, and do it in several languages too. On a visit to Auschwitz, for example, he managed to offend the Jews. He injured them still further when he said that abortion was a far worse act than the holocaust. But for sheer, naked meddling in politics, look at the visit he made to Croatia. It being a Catholic state and the others all being Orthodox or Muslim, he more or less told them to become the beacon of faith in Europe. To what extent precisely is he the fuse that lit the terrible civil war?

I do not know the answer. I do know that the Vatican has a

---

2. I quote from the insert of a cassette called "Le Rock'N'Roll - Viol de la conscience" (Rock 'n Roll: The Rape of the Conscience) presented by Father Jean-Paul Régimbal of Quebec, and distributed and produced by Les Editions Saint-Raphaël, Geneva, Switzerland. "In Spring '82, the group Led Zeppelin was condemned by a tribunal in California for passing subliminal messages of a satanic character in its disc "Stairway to Heaven".

huge group of diplomats and a P.R. centre which would do credit to any maker of soap powder. It washes cleaner too. By anyone's standard, one has got to admit that the Pope has not had a very good year. I haven't even mentioned affairs in the Baltic States, the Ukraine, the Lebanon, the city of Belfast, Corsica, Africa or Manila. The church says that she strives for peace. That is the posture she adopts.

But before the onset of the Second World War, she entered into a concordat with Adolf Hitler. She pledged not to obstruct him in any way, so long as he did not touch church property or personnel. This is why the War Cabinet felt obliged to consult the church before giving the green light for Operation Mistletoe ... the one which persuaded Rudolf Hess to abandon Hitler. But one has only to inspect a map of the world and it becomes quite clear. Where the church is, there too is turmoil.

Links

Jesus said: "When you hurt one of my little ones ... better you were thrown into the sea." The church says: "The Holy Father runs the whole church and cannot concern himself with individual cases." So who is counting the hairs on our heads today? Who makes a note of each sparrow that falls? Ever since the church was founded, it has been the direct cause of huge amounts of suffering. It meddled in the politics of so many states, it virtually ruled Europe. It butchered heretics, it condemned the Jews, it mounted crusades, and it trained the Order of Preachers to be its experts on torture.

Today it may be far less frontal but it still wreaks damage behind the scenes - and always in the name of the faith. Take birth control for instance - does anyone truly think that all the faithful in Europe are obeying the church rules? Rates of birth are falling even in Catholic countries. By pure chance, of course, levels of church attendance are dropping rapidly, and there are not enough new priests. Would anyone care to count the number of disused churches or the parishes that have had to be 'joined' together?

Well, one could say that the Pope has a right to govern the church as he sees fit. But how far may he go? Does he have the right to forbid condoms *even to prevent AIDS*? When the disease is pandemic, will the International Court of Justice condemn him?

151

At least he can say that the Bishops of Ireland don't use them either. Other sects are even more severe. The Law has had to be used against parents who refuse urgent surgical treatment for their children. It is lunatic to let gays die because you don't like their sexual habits.

The church doesn't much care for any form of sexual pleasure. Even married couples are told to think of babies, though I doubt if many of them do. In fact, the thought of babies would turn most men impotent with panic ... which may be the real point of it all! Anyway, is this attitude toward 'gays' any different from sewing pink triangles on their sleeves and sending them to death camps?

Don't jump to the wrong idea. I do not condone sexual deviance. But the point is not whether it is evil but that it is an even greater evil to let people die simply because you view them as sinners. It's no help to say there were gay priests, gay bishops and even gay popes. A celibate church, like the boy scout movement or the army, is a good place to hide such things. That is all one can honestly say about it. On the other hand, the church keeps strange friends for a body that is simply spiritual.

Italy, for example, is not just the H.Q. for the Roman Catholic church. It is also the home of the Mafia, the Comora, the Masonic P2 Lodge, and the largest Communist party outside Russia! One way or another, the Vatican or its bank has tangled with all of them. We cannot mock the extreme sects who say the Pope is the Devil. Neither can we mock the Pope for saying he's Christ's Vicar on earth. Neither side has solid evidence, so neither has sued the other for slander. One must judge men by their deeds.

This is why certain events make me wonder about the church's kinship with the devil. You see, most other creeds have allowed poor old Satan to languish in neglect. They do not talk about him. They do not invite him to dinner. But the Catholic church not only keeps him alive - *it has a vested interest in doing so*.

Nothing fills up a church quite so quickly as terror! I'll return to this point later, but in the meantime think of all those films from Hollywood: little girls who vomit bile, living dead, haunted houses, and diabolic attacks. Have you never noticed that only a *'real priest'* can exorcise the evil? Clearly, we are being told to choose between four options:-

1. Only the church has any real authority over these entities from hell.

2. That is precisely what the church would like the world to believe. So it pays tribute to these entities to get them to play the game.

3. Although highly addictive, the films are total rubbish, but they do the church no harm at all and are tolerated.

4. One way or another the public is being taken for a ride. Its myths, its ignorance and its fears are being brutally exploited!

Which, or how many of these, would you put your money on? Dear old Aleister Crowley knew the answer, and the answer is no great compliment to Christians in general or any of the separate churches.

The Devil & Aleister Crowley

There are many devout Christians. Some of them are so zealous that they financed and produced a recent television feature which purported to expose "Satanic child abuse". But not having access to any real events, they wrote their own script and employed actors to perform the roles. Of course, part of the programme claimed that these people were followers of my father's teachings. Not only that, they also said my father was born in Scotland![3]

I think this is a perfect example of their own morality. When they hate, they are prepared to lie and commit sin - just as in the past they were prepared to torture and kill. These bigots are not as far removed from Papistry as they like to imagine. Nor is their way of behaving all that far from Black Magic. In fact, to be quite frank, doesn't all this smell somewhat of the Nazis and their campaign of hate against the Jews? They said they ate babies, you know!

Evidently, there are sincere and well-bred people about who, never having met Crowley, are willing to adopt the myths and use him as what the Americans call "a fall-guy". They chuck him to the lions instead of treating him as a living star. As in the fantasy industry, so in real life. To make a point, one simply grabs someone (dead, if possible) and forces him into the role of the

---

3. The whole sordid affair was exposed by'"The Daily Mail'. Friends of my own, who work in television too, tried to contact the producers of this cultural masterpiece but, as usage has it, they were unavailable for comment. I suspect they had gone on a week-end retreat to consult more closely with their God. I hope they remembered me in their prayers. I did not forget them.

153

villain so that the whole congregation can boo aloud and feel good. That's how it has always been. Despite the death of Jesus Christ, his own followers have not much changed.[4] How then can I hope to change them?

As regards my books and my teaching, most folk scoff or pretend that I do not exist. I do not blame them. If I were in their shoes, I would probably do the same. Although I'd show a bit more tact and not display my wounds. This is why my enemies stay calm, smile broadly, and pretend that every set-back was just part of the plan. "When it comes to playing poker, they are the Masters!" That is how Aleister put it.

He also thought that the Devil got the trick from us. We must have taught him because he couldn't have found it out for himself. At the time, he was speaking in metaphors of course. Right then and there he was not stating that the Devil, as such, was real. He was talking about the general belief in him, and the qualities that folk attribute to him.

According to my father, the process of "*altering Old Nick*" got under way during the 18th century, and was a late result of the Reformation. All at once, the Devil was sacked! People were bored by him. They began to lose interest in him. The Devil went out of fashion. "He must have been deeply hurt," said Aleister, eyes twinkling. "There are not many mystical entities who find they are out of work at his age!"

Needless to say, the devil is a very lively chap. He did not get as high as he did without a modicum of talent! So although fewer people felt menaced, he had some strength left - like chasing a crippled nun or bringing down a scruffy hermit who'd eaten mouldy bread[5]. But despite all his efforts to stage a come-back, the bottom fell out of the market and the Fallen Angel fell yet again. There was a sharp, ninety per cent drop in demonic seizures, which was very bad news indeed for all experts in exorcism.

4. If we want to talk about child abuse, would anyone like to discuss The Children's Crusade? In the 13th century tens of thousands of French and German children set off "to save Jerusalem". The majority were captured and sold into slavery, while others were killed and piled up in mountains of bones. (cf. Peter de Rosa, "Vicars of Christ", 1988). This, by the way, is the true origin of the legend of the Pied Piper of Hamelin.
5. St Anthony, the first hermit, and the supposed founder of monasticism, suffered from terrible visions. But modern scientists have attributed these "temptations" to his habit of eating old bread - bread that was infected by the fungus claviceps purpurea that contains lysergic acid, the substance from which L.S.D. is made.

Their union did all it could to bolster trade, naturally. They smuggled the devil into the odd convent now and then, or the random stately home, or even stray lunatic asylums. A bottle of absinthe was very good, in this respect. More recently, I hear they are using drugs called *ecstasy* or *angels wings*. But it was all to no avail. It was quite obvious to everybody that dear, old Satan was on his very last legs.

The Lumière brothers gave him the kiss of life with their work on moving pictures. Films have achieved a hyper realism that gets better all the time. Anyone can watch weird events in the High Street. We can feel the thrills of violence, horror, sex and torture. The devil has stock in the amusement industry.

I'm not saying that he did it all legally. After all, he is a champion cheat and trickster. Like a *Legend of Hollywood*, Satan has worked for the prestige he won. Unlike the others though, he is alive and kicking! I hear he has a bijou apartment in the London suburb of Camden, and a studio near Pigalle in Paris.

But he is not the star that he used to be.

21

APEDAMAK

The lion god of battle

The Bead Game

In philology, the science of languages, one speaks of "*the T shift*", or "*the s elision*". Over the centuries, you see, a language tends to get ironed out and the phonemes that are more difficult to pronounce become squashed or cut. In this way we can compute how one word, in Persian say, became another word in English.[1] Since the changes always move in the same direction, one that makes speaking easier, not only can we discover the rules ... we can now trace words back to their earlier forms and rebuild a 'lost' language.

Something along the same lines can be applied to the study of magic, ritual and religion. Here too, there is a similar kind of gradual dilution or decay. If one takes a closer look at my father's ideas on ritual, for instance, they were more complex than a mere almanac of liturgical colours. In the Catholic Church, the priests wear red vestments on the feast of a martyr, white on the feasts of a virgin, green, purple, black and so on. In other words, although the Mass is the same in all these cases, the minor details are changed. The effect is to add to the human interest. It makes people feel more 'in the know'. But it does not add anything to the 'spiritual value' of the ritual.

In great religions[2], the trivia have grown in emphasis, while the crucial elements have shrunk, and in some cases faded away. One very clear case is the Shinto religion of Japan, and another is the Anglican Church. For example, should Christians try to follow the same religion that Jesus Christ himself followed ... which was

---

1. Yes, it may sound absurd, but English and Persian are members of the same family of languages, along with Faroese, Icelandic and Dutch.
2. I am using the term "church" in the scientific sense, i.e., in the sense that a church is an international organization with central control.

Judaism of a special shade? The notion of a Redeemer and Atonement did not exist before Him but have been adopted since. Take a sacrament, for example: each church makes its own kind of ritual which is pinned in place by a spot of imitative magic. In it, one portrays a life or a story and one hopes for a specific effect or outcome.

So it is in occult ritual and magic. Most of the important things have been 'lost' over the years, and the 'central act' has stepped sideways. *There has been a shift of focus from the crux to the fringes, from the essence to the edges.* Man has added, man has adorned, man has sought to 'improve'. The result has been a kind of *organized* or *managed* occultism. Let us not forget that the origins of European theatre lie in the ancient rituals of Greece. What was mystical has now become a stage show. In other cases it has become a game, a folk-song or a children's ring dance.

Like Baroness Rothschild's little finger when drinking tea, one has lost sight of the true purpose - which is thirst.

To cut a long story short, when dealing with the ethereal, one's methods start to solidify. The original breadth and richness of the ritual language becomes sorted into its various elements. These are then more finely sliced into tinier cabinets where they become the nuts and bolts of the business. This is like the tired chic of 18th century drama, where trainees learned set postures from which any drama could be built. In other words, there is no freedom.

It is now taboo to follow one's impulses. Everything is as tight and regular as the ticking of a clock, but there is a certain tension in the air. After all, the formula might work just as they said it would. The hour might yet strike! Can you imagine what would happen if the faithful came together, called on their God - and He answered?

I suppose that what I'm saying is: ritual tends to become stilted - one might even say fossilized. It loses a great deal of the initial sense and natural impulse, and there remains only a stiff outer form which is bereft of magical content. The managers want to be in control, you see, and they can't afford to risk oracles coming down on just anyone. They want no excess, no charisma, and no one talking direct to the Beyond.

On the one hand, a simple but genuine ritual can elevate one's soul to a new level of knowing. On the other hand, complex

157

ritual is more likely to provoke esteem for the beauty of the spectacle. Like a plain, peasant burial, the one brings awe. Like the one and only film called 'Cleopatra', the other brings an attack of sensory upheaval.

The Board

Crowley, the actor manqué, was very drawn to the stately type of ritual, very close to classic theatre. He would not have liked either to improvise or to take part in Dionysiac riots. He was smart enough to see this tendency in his own character. It is the same kind of mental rigidity which pushes eggheads to the Left and workers to the extreme Right. Like many other people before him and since, Aleister Crowley could not abide people who were too similar to himself. He knew it. What's more, he even knew the reason for it: he was afraid that their presence might release a part of his character that he had problems keeping under control.

This special feature has been given a wide spectrum of names, such as divine madness, the Holy Ghost, or just plain ecstasy. It depends on the context, which word you choose. Crowley very rarely 'let it rip'. He preferred to stay under control. Perhaps it was a legacy from the years in the Plymouth Brethren. It certainly wasn't timidity, neither was it any fear of looking like a fool.[3] I think he knew that in order to re-order the world, one must so dismantle it that one comes uneasily close to chaos again. Just like any student of the mystic, he didn't quite have the courage to fling himself into the unknown. The mind of each human being contains 'something' which, rather like plutonium, can approach a state of 'critical mass'. One needs a ritual to get closer.

As he himself once said: "*I was not put here to be King among the donkeys, nor to be a slave who adds a few more stones to the pyramid. I was intended to understand the purpose of Self and then go beyond it.*"

This is why there are so many stories about him. This is why he went ahead with such silly rituals. There were lots of toadies among his small band of allies. He was never one to like a long cortege, so even a single sponger would have weighed heavily in the balance, so to speak. One other upshot was that, being fools, they blabbed. The wiser ones kept quiet, of course. They were the ones who acted like a catalyst and in their company Crowley

---

3. Just think of some of the photographs that he posed for!

found that his powers were "enabled". Since they helped him to achieve his own majesty, he revealed some of the mystery to their eyes, and naturally they never spoke.

The Plan

Later on, I noticed that AC's views were close to those of modern science as regards the implied origin of the mystical urge. Social science looks for the function of things, what purpose they serve and what good they do. But the Pilgrim cannot stand so aloof from the truth. He is biased. He has a certain motive for what he does. So whereas the scholar wants to find out: how, why and what, the Pilgrim wants merely to be. Yet both of them see ritual as something that began in the distant past.

It was a primeval urge that man should bear witness to his mission by climbing out of the mud. But far more than this, man was nearing a state in which planned changes could take place. It was for him to open the way to further changes that would succeed in due time. He had to take that next step, for the gods demanded it. Here, we find a similar element at work in many kinds of magic. These stages of development, each dependent on the one previous, are often referred to as The Seven Keys. In a way they are similar to 'chinese boxes', one being hidden inside another, or else the 'turns' in a labyrinth. It is worth reminding you at this point that the human body purports to have seven 'vital centres'.

He had to go on since their Plan depended on his nature as a vehicle for headway. The plan did not open out as if one were unfolding a map. It was much more akin to the gradual unfolding of a flower inside a rosebud. Note the frequent reference in Crowleyan magic to the butterfly and the chrysalis as symbols of the "pure one" emerging from the "ugly one".

Yes, man was daunted by the unknown, but no more than we might be today when defying a ghastly disease such as AIDS. He was at his weakest during the night, when his most critical faculty, sight, was more or less reduced to nothing. With no optical cues to guide him, he trusted in wariness and, over thousands of years, this has become psychic fear and anxiety now.

His dreams of terror were far worse than reality, but his visions of paradise were far nobler too. Perhaps it was just a Land of Dreams or a sort of early Cockaigne? This is an old word for an ideal town of London and it comes from the Old French: pais de cocaigne, meaning 'the Land of Cakes'. Before the days of public transport, this must have been how people thought of the great city. But then, when I think about it again, perhaps Crowley's "lack of unbelief" allowed him to make contact with a greater source of help?

On the whole, social science accepts that people with a spiritual faith are more proof against any psychic illness, than those who have not.[4] It could just be the 'magic rabbit's foot' effect, of course. It could all be an old wives' tale. The point is though that his whole being benefits. A sceptic will say that the good results are due to the power of the healer's 'prestige'. But in that case, why can the same result not be obtained in sceptics? There is a contrast, it seems, between those who trust in science and those who trust in God. Which is another way of saying that: what does the trick is something which doesn't exist in the material sense.

The Notion of Soul

The great Emile Durkheim[5], and other students of society, opined that early man stumbled on the concept of 'soul' as a result of dreaming. Of course, no one has yet provided a cogent explanation of what kind of process dreaming might truly be. Come to that, nobody knows what sleep is, yet we are terribly familiar with it. We spend one third of our life enjoying it!

Despite this, Early Man noticed that during his dreams he met, spoke to and had contact with other persons many of whom he greeted, but some of whom were unknown. Other men pointed out that they had met him. Yet each had taken his turn at look-out, and all vowed that sleeping persons did not walk, talk, or go anywhere. They therefore reasoned that man has a vapoury double which quits the body via the nostrils, flies at immense speed, and uses immense forces. In time, this 'other self' developed into the concept of a spirit or soul.

It was also obvious that people sometimes had dreams from which they did not waken. When that happened the fleshy part of the self began to corrupt. This, plus the fact that thwacks on the head dropped folk senseless, implied that the soul's link with home could be snapped. They tried to imagine where these

4. cf. Michael Argyle, 'Religious Behaviour', London 1958.
5. The French sociologist, Durkheim 1858-1917

absent souls were kept. Plainly then, whatever the link might be, it was certainly not permanent because the soul could come and go as it willed. So there grew the notion of trance states and ecstasy. This term comes from the Greek and means "being out of the body".

All too often so-called mystics take this to mean either a kind of divine or mystic infusion or some sort of exalted and ineffable joy. While both those conditions can be achieved, the fact of ecstasy is something close to the idea of "free, detached, available or eligible". The more intently they thought about it, the clearer it became that the linkage with life was very frail and various things could shatter it. Man began to ask where that soul was when not in its correct mansion. He was curious about reaching out to vagrant souls such as his departed kinsmen with no body to come back to.

The Lodger

Once outside the cage of flesh, they were also beyond the rule of time. Once all tethers were cut, they had access to energies unavailable to men who clung to their bones. Clearly, it was in man's best interests if he could touch this mystical potential and perhaps have use of it. Naturally, one began with the souls that were closest, i.e, one's own dead, or the ancients of one's tribe. At first glance, this looks like a selfish attempt to win profit. But at a hermetic level, it was a blessed liaison like that called "*the communion of saints*".

Crowley did not believe that any of this could have been pure chance. It came about because The Source called to men in the stillness of their hearts. The event was too recent to have caused genetic change. It had nothing to do with Jungian ideas on racial memory or the group unconscious, even if this was quite a winsome theory. One must not be so reckless as to endorse ideas just because they fit in with one's existing ideas and opinions.

A faint likeness is not the same thing as strong evidence, nor is an intense sympathy any kind of proof. To find truth we must be more critical of ourselves, of our ways of thinking, and of the contents of our minds. Aleister Crowley, my father, believed that all such lofty, or mystic concepts, had to be older than man. It was possible that they had existed in an earlier kind of hominid and carried over to us.

This is very unlikely since no species before our own ever showed respect for the dead or made any attempt to bury them. It follows that Homo Sapiens was the first to know about soul. In which case, all men, at all periods, have had the same religious tendency. This is why Crowley argued that it must have been revealed. In short, there had been an Epiphany and, very possibly, an on-going and endless "walk with the Gods".

What the Gods gave was Will. The crowning of that Will was the power to conceive an image and make that image real. More than stars; Crowley held that man and woman were destined to be Gods. Did he mean that we are made of the same substance?[6] Or are we simply absorbed, like water into dry rice, to achieve a state that is conjoint with godhood? We need a lexicon of our own. But it is axiomatic that truth should be open to all men, with or without 'good' education.

Early ritual was mimicry of action. But fixation on deed soon faded, and meaning was stated in magical ways. Thus dumbness and unknowing had an effect like that of 'isolation tanks', which demonstrates how sensory poverty can expose the deeper layers of a brain. When language came, it never made ritual redundant. Some rituals add pomp to a civic occasion, but others give access to other realities. The 'right way' to perform ritual grew over the years, along with the right sound, gesture, movement and aims. Thus, Man not only contacted the 'gods'; he brought back a little of their power.

He forgot he'd done it better in the beginning.

6. i.e. consubstantial, as are the Father, Son and Holy Ghost in most branches of Christianity.

162

22

MEHEN

The coiled serpent who protects the sun-god, Ra

The Cathars

The simple word 'becoming' does not convey very much - or at least, not when it is put like that, out of nowhere and apropos of nothing. Whereas there is a useful term which exists in the special language of philosophy, which is often called The Queen of Sciences. The term I am referring to is "*entelechy*"[1] which means "*to make one's potential real*". In occultism, we tend to look at it more as a process than a state of being, but we soon change our opinions once it has been achieved.

In other words, that which has been only possible now comes into existence and is. We could also call it a triumph of self, except that this carries an allusion to talent, hope or ambition. This notion of entelechy has always been at the heart of mystic thought. It is clearly implied in the recurring reference to clarity of vision e.g, "*A fool sees not the same tree that a wise man sees*".[2] There is an even more famous passage from the same author: "*If the doors of perception were cleansed, everything would appear as it is, infinite*".

Today, the Church of Dianetics (once known as Scientology and the cause of much disquiet) speaks of "Clears". The very word Buddha means 'Who Has Seen Light'. An Iranian proverb asks: "What does the blind man see in the stars?" In the Book of Isaiah, the prophet says: "The people that walked in darkness have seen a great light."

In many parts of mediaeval Europe there was a sect which was declared heretic by the church. This was the Cathars, whose name means "*the pure ones*" or perhaps "*those who have been*

1. This comes from the Greek "entelekheia",*en*, in, *telos*, perfection, end, *echein*, to have.
2. William Blake, 1757-1827, "A Memorable Fancy".

cleansed". Of course, there were other names too, such as the Bogomils, or the Albigenses, and many more abusive tags. Although the sect flowered around the year 1140, their true origin lay with the much older Gnostic faith.

The Cathars believed in two opposed forces of good and evil, each of which posed a constant threat to the other. The good principle was of course God, but the evil principle was known as *The Monster of Chaos*. It was believed that the Monster of Chaos partook of the nature of man, and so man's task was to liberate his own spirit - or cleanse himself.

When Aleister Crowley took on the title "*The Great Beast 666*", he was in fact defying the forces of chaos. He was more or less saying: "Wyatt Earp? Wyatt Earp? I'm the new Wyatt Earp!" In other words he was uttering a challenge to the Monster and declaring that he, Crowley, had begun the journey toward gnosis.

It is worth noting too that when the crusade began, the Cathar men were often tortured by having great nails hammered through their sexual parts. This says as much about Dominican monks as the horror of the Death Camps said about the S.S. They said that the reason for this form of torture was that Cathar men had also been accused of sodomy.[3] They said the same thing about the Templars, a little later. It was one of those charges designed to raise the gorge among the faithful. It was like breeding hatred for the Jews by saying "they eat babies". But there was, and is, a much more fundamental reason why the church lambasts this thing they call sodomy.

I quote from the Bible: "*I am distressed for thee, my brother Jonathan: very pleasant hast thou been unto me: thy love to me was wonderful, passing the love of women.*"[4] Yet in the Pentateuch, indeed in Genesis itself, the twin cities of the plains, called Sodom and Gomorrah, are destroyed because of men seeking "to know" (carnally) the sons of others. Well, King David has a special place in Jewish hearts because he saved Israel when he slew Goliath. But not only that, by the time the Book of Samuel was written, King Solomon had met and been influenced by the Queen of Sheba.

3. In current English there is a defamatory term, bugger, which means either the act of sodomy or one who commits it. It came into our language from Old French, "bougre", which simply meant "a heretic". This in turn derives from the Latin "bulgarus" which was a neutral, non-pejorative term for referring to the Greek Church, rather than the Roman one.

4. 2 Samuel: 1:25.

The church wished to soft pedal the fact that Jesus was unmarried. It was awkward to explain that he went around with twelve male disciples. It called for neat footwork to account for his words that no man had greater love than to die for his friends.

The Cathar name for a man or woman, who had taken the step from "*being capable of doing*" to "*having done*" was "*A Perfect*". This epithet did not portray any kind of ideal soul, nor yet a special man who was already one with God. It meant a person who was now '*absolute*'. Whatever bad he had done, whatever good he had not done, he had cleaned away all trace of impurity. A great deal might still be lacking but - everything inside his soul was proper and right.

To put it more simply, a Perfect was on his way, but he had not necessarily arrived. His being was 'like' God. But he was not yet one with God. He was getting ready for that next step: a very real "*alchymic wedding*" into which would be born "*a third substance*".

The Cathars were not a casual, one-off event. Their truth existed before them and it lives on after them. The truth was not in them but they in it. They had no fear of evil, not because they were stronger but because evil attacks only what it might vanquish - the souls of dubiety. *Those who have rendered to Truth are no longer fair game.*

The Sleeping Truth
No, Crowley did not seek to revive the Cathars in general, nor to commend any special detail of their belief or praxis. Indeed, it has to be said that the original Cathars might very well have been daunted by his unique views on sex. But then again, there is some evidence to suggest that they might not! Whatever the reasons for an onslaught by the church, she would go to any lengths to justify her deeds by painting the victims as black as possible. One of the usual charges was that they had sexual congress with the devil, than which nothing more horrific could be imagined.

But for their part, the Cathars were just as outraged by church excesses as well as her sexual perjury. Pope Innocent III issued a Bull of Anathema but the King of France refused to lead a crusade against the Cathars. As head of his army, the Pope had to nominate the head of a new order of monks. These were sons

165

of St Benedict who had set up their centre at Citeaux[5], near Dijon. No one has been able to estimate how many hundreds of thousands of simple people were murdered at that time.

I referred earlier to a crypt in which many of the Cathar perfecti sleep a just sleep. This is, of course, the Cave of Ornolhac. It lies above the river Ariège very close to the point where it is joined by the waters of Ussat. The mouth of the cave lies roughly half-way up the rugged gorge which hugs the river. It is known that it was an important site for druidic rites, being suspended, so to speak, between water and air.

There is a strong belief, I put it no stronger than that, that the 'truth' had been brought to the Cathars by the Bulgarian Initiate, called Nicetas. One may speculate endlessly about the unknown Master of the Cathars[6] and even whether any such person existed. It seems obvious that the Cathar beliefs did not just arrive *off the cuff*.

If real scholars would read their texts more carefully, they would see that Crowley was closer to the Cathar position than they thought. For the Cathars did not view one's sexual nature as a scourge. Nor was it a millstone to be tied round the neck. Used properly it was a flowery crown to be worn in purity and pride. Still, Crowley's view of sex and magic must be dealt with later. I can give you a précis though:-

"It is white magic when you use the power caringly and have the authority to do so. It is black magic when you use it for selfish reasons and rely on the authority of force. The human mind, remember, can believe that black is white, and white is black. So how can I be certain that I know which is which? Until he appears before a higher court, I can only judge a man by his actions."

The Dodderer

What did AC do in his declining years? It would be more apposite to ask first if he did in fact decline! Colin Wilson, (who never met Crowley), thinks he produced some good poetry. John Symonds[7] who did meet him in 1940, found him old, bored, rather pathetic, thin and dried up. Apart from pathetic, which is Mr Symonds' own feeling, I am not too worried about his choice of words.

My father was aged sixty-five, we must remember, and living

5.   whence their new name, the Cistercians.

on meagre food rations, just like anybody else. He also endured quite serious asthma and the outcome was that he was also a drug addict. If anyone hoped he might be an Olympic athlete, they must have been cracked. Strange to say, I found him larger, livelier and in much finer fettle than Mr Symonds did. Granted, mine was a child's point of view, but it was also a much closer look.

Our last meeting was in 1944, when there were only three more years left to him. If those other authors and I are all telling the truth, which is not impossible, then a new question arises. Which of us was Crowley deceiving? And what might his reasons have been?

Many authors write about my father's life - far too many, in my opinion. Their works meet much the same reaction, which is small wonder, noticing how they restate much the same thing. Even when there is no solid grounds whatever for asserting something, one author will simply quote from another. Or else they will use weasel phrases such as "*Mrs. Simpson once said*", and "a *friend of his brother who happened to be passing the window*" etc. There are ways of turning innuendo into fact, are there not? But he is a popular subject and most of the books usually sell well.

Ah well! Whatever such writers may believe or say, the medical men who attended to Crowley knew enough about asthma to provide the drugs that he needed. In those days, they recognized the fact that he would die without them. There was no prospect of curing him because other doctors, back in the 19th century, had given him drugs in childhood. To begin with it was laudanum, also known as Tincture of Poppies, and very popular with artists.

The doctor gave the script only to satisfy Crowley's mother. It wasn't really essential since medicines of this type could be bought over the counter in any chemist's shop. It is quite illegal now, of course, but in those days laudanum was as common as aspirin. It was taken by both rich and poor alike. It seems to have done no great damage either. The general use of opiates didn't stop the great Empire from growing nor halt the spread of industry.

Even today, addiction to drugs is seen as an illness and not as a flagrant evil. The real culprits are the criminal elements who

6. see: Maurice Magre, 'The Return of the Magi', Philip Allan Ltd, London 1981.
7. John Symonds, 'The Magick of Aleister Crowley', Frederick Muller Ltd. 1958.

167

traffic in drugs, many of them coming from the poorer states in South America. As is the case with the Mafia and Sicily, organized crime does seem to be more common in Catholic countries. The only explanation that has been offered so far comes from Max Weber's finding of a curious link between the Protestant ethic and Capitalism.

In any case, being Crowley's son, I can throw a little more light on the subject than most other people. He did not hide his habit from me. He simply forbade me ever to touch drugs myself. I am almost the age at which Mr. Symonds met my father. I look as my father did in the prime of his life: a big man, a rotund man, a hairy man, complete with asthma. Not unlike the Yeti, in fact.

Crowley was cautious of his old friends and had long since begun to hide things from them. He was dependent on their help, of course, and was careful not to offend them. Some, like Gerald Yorke and Karl Germer, were very fond of him and he was properly grateful. But he knew they would look askance at any more of his "wheezes", which is how they viewed many of his magical acts.

He was also dubious about the younger element who might yet paint a red-nose on his corpse and make his name a mockery. I don't think he was too worried about someone else making a fortune out of his name. What's more, neither I nor any of his other children would want to change any of the designs he made as regards his own writings. Having been born a bastard, there's not a lot one could do anyway. As for the others, they hide behind the sandbags lest the 'gentlemen of the press' start shooting again.

His Final Acts

He would not have liked the slant that friends have put on his work. He would not have approved the way they re-told the story in the way the world wanted to hear it. Even if all the myths and scandals were true, and they are not, they have nothing whatever to do with Crowley's teaching. It is all very well for priests to propose that God made sex but it exists in us only as a remnant of our animal origins. But we are animals. We are the most developed species among them, but not a creature apart. Do you truly think it would fulfil God's plan, to build "a new Jerusalem" so to speak, if we disown the bed-rock and the footing? We are the only creature to have altered brute noise into

168

poetry. We have changed the hunt into a culinary art. We no longer sleep in chance caves or grottoes but build arches[8] of marble. Where ninety per cent of babies once died in childhood, more than ninety per cent now live. And we have changed sex from a seasonal rut into a kind of social mortar that holds marriage, family and village life together. Not only that. What honours can we offer the Gods when all that we possess was given to us by them? Our eldest son? Yes, that is a token. Our yearling lamb? Yes, that too is a token. Bread and wine perhaps? Yes, that is a token of a token, *a sacrifice at second remove.* Then why not proffer the hope of our posterity, as the bible puts it?

"As for the Future," says Antoine de St Exupéry, "your task is not to foresee, but to enable it."[9]

Or as Crowley said: "*How dare we see ourselves with shame? It is a fact that we are glorious. It is a fact that we may recreate that glory. When acting as channels of cosmic power, where is the wrong in the gods ravishing our souls?*"

These words cast new light on the Law of Thelema. "Do what thou wilt is the whole of the Law. Love is the Law, Love under the Will."

Those who thought they knew it all, know almost nothing at all.

---

8. This is the real meaning of the word "architecture".
9. Saint-Exupéry, 'The Wisdom of the Sands', 1948 (trans. Stuart Gilbert).

23
LUG

A Celtic god. Also known as "he whose hands reach everywhere" because of his association with magic and sunlight

Death

Each head has its own mythology. Inside most human minds the Land of Evil, Hell, Gehenna or Hades is always located at the spot where we bury our dead. If you think about it, it does seem fairly logical. Had we sealed our dead in titanium caskets and launched them into space, then hell would almost certainly have been 'up there'. It is a fact of simple gravity though that when someone feels ill, their legs give way, and they sink to the bed or the earth. When they have died we cannot exactly hang them up on coat-hooks or tie them to a chair at the dinner table, so we dispose of them. It is this manner of disposal that determines our ideas about the after-life.

"Many people panic", said Crowley, "because death so often comes as a surprise. Even when they are very old, or when they have been sick for years ... it is a state to which they do not really manage to adapt themselves. So even *they* may feel a momentary terror." He smoothed his hair back – oh yes, he no longer bothered to shave his skull, and he refused to pay for something as simple as that.

"It is such a shame, don't you think? Even when pious Christians go forth like valiant soldiers to confront their Judge – it reminds me a bit of pigs being pushed into a sausage machine." He did not laugh. "The priests, the professionals, utter their formula and tell you to get off the train calmly and quietly. But ... you look at them. You wonder. And a voice whispers in your ear. That last sign said 'Auschwitz', didn't it?"

He sighed and gripped my hand. "We are meant to prepare ourselves. Would a butterfly every emerge if the chrysalis passed the time playing a mouth-organ?" He arrumphed, gently. "No

170

matter how young, no matter how old, each one of us should be ready for the transfer."

I remember thinking how silly it seemed, to entertain such morbid thoughts when you were as young and nippy as me. Why on earth should a boy of ten turn his thoughts to death? We were excused, weren't we? Children didn't die, did they? And even if they did, the people 'over their' would help us.

"You think that," he said telepathically, "because no one has ever spoken to you about it. If you were to belong to another people, in another time, you would probably be in a monastery getting ready for adolescence."

"Is adolescence so much like Death," I asked pertly.

"It is the time when most people begin to die," he replied.

The Magick Diaries

Much has been made of Crowley's magical diaries. Even the gentle, objective Gerald Yorke believed what Crowley told him, i.e. that certain signs meant an act of masturbation, while others meant sexual intercourse with penetration, buggery, defloration of a virgin etc. I am afraid that this is not quite true. Nowhere in Crowley's teachings does there exist any statement to suggest that *every* sexual act, of no matter what kind, could accumulate power. Why then would he keep such a detailed record of his libidinous deeds?

The truth is that these symbols actually represent something else. They stand for magical acts – and magical acts which do not necessarily include any sexual activity. They might well, of course, if the ritual to which he refers required a sexual charge. But Crowley was not keeping a schoolboy's record of how many times he did it or how far he could ejaculate! He was keeping a log of sacred activities which he performed in a certain sequence, and at a certain frequency, in order to achieve some higher, supernatural objective by a certain date. You can see the diaries at the Warburg Institute in London. If you apply an objective eye and a soupçon of mathematics, you will be able to fathom the patterns. What you will not find is the actual meaning of the symbols.

In his book 'Aleister Crowley – The Nature of the Beast', Colin Wilson attacks my father from every direction at the same time. On p.43 he quotes from Crowley's 'Aceldama' and then passes the following comment: "It is, in fact, a typical Crowleyan rhapsody to sin, whoredom and degradation." That may well be so, but it would carry a great deal more meaning to someone who had heard about what is called "the whore wisdom" of the Christian epoch. If you check your dictionary, you will find that the word 'magdalen' means 'a reformed prostitute'. You will also find, with very little research, that the gnostic term 'sophia' is also given as 'prunikos' which means 'lewd'. In the Gnostic Gospel of Philip, Mary Magdalen is described as "the woman who knew all."

Not to put too fine a point on it, the Gnostics regards sex as beneficial to those who understood its significance. They believed that Christ was the Child of Sophia (wisdom and lewdness) and Bythos (meaning depth, profundity). In St Matthew's gospel, which used to be called 'The Book of The Genealogy of Jesus Christ', several whores are listed *as being ancestors of Christ*. There are four ladies called Tamar, Rahab, Ruth and Bathsheba. In Alexandria, Mary herself was accused of conceiving Jesus by her own brother, or to a lover called Pandira. As the Gnostic Gospel of Philip puts it: "His sister and his mother and his companion were all a Mary."

The upshot of all this is that Aleister Crowley was not just another magician or occultist. He belonged to a school of thought that pre-dates Christianity and even Judaism itself. It was a religion in which, for instance, each person would "...*wisely take the measure of his breasts and balance this against the weight of his sex. For he must not be what he is not, but become what he always was...*"[1]

All religion has an origin, whatever that might be. Sociologists have one idea, followers of the Jungian school have another, and the religious themselves have a third. But just as Thomas Acquinas used the universality of the religious impulse as one of his proofs for the existence of God, imagine how much stronger and more devastating the argument would be if one could demonstrate that *all* religions were descended from the *same* source! That is my position. That was Crowley's position. That has been the position of true Masters since the beginnings of time.

"To achieve the fulfilment of self," said Aleister, "you need to

1. This is a quotation from 'The Book of Desolation'.

know three things. First, you must know where you are at this moment. Second, you must know your proper destination. Third, you must have a map which lets you make sense of the other two things." Then he would add with his typical twinkle: "Who you are and what you are called matter not one twitter!"

Sea-level and Such

"We are not descended from slugs," said Crowley. "Oh, well, one or two perhaps, but it will always be marked in their passports!"[2] He folded the fingers of his two hands and laid them on his stomach. "It is not in our nature to grub tunnels in the earth and hide away from danger. Not that the soil is all that free of danger anyway. There are moles and other unpleasant things. Not to mention the entities from Beyond who behave very much like ant-eaters."

"Men are divided into two sorts. There are those who clamp their jaws together whenever their mouth is closed, and there are others whose lips touch but not their teeth. This is not very important in itself. But it becomes significant when there is a sudden change of habit such as when a jaw unexpectedly clenches or when it sags." Crowley was a tight-jawed man. Now, as he launched into a 'lesson', his jaw sagged, and I saw his face in a new light. It was as if all pretensions had been dropped as well and the tissues of his face and skull simply showed the bone structure underneath. For a moment, he had let his mask slip.

"We are meant to go high, and higher still," he said. "We hauled ourselves out of the primordial slime, but this, the earth, was not intended to be the end of our journey. They want us to go higher. They want us to live there, where it is not the most easeful for our bones."

I wanted to butt in and ask "Where is that?", but I thought better of it. If I made any comment or did anything to interrupt his 'flow', there was always the risk he would lose his train of thought. He could speak, off the cuff, for hours at a time. He didn't need any notes or references by his side. He could 'see' his subject in his head, as if it existed in real space – as if it were a maquette built in all three dimensions. He knew beforehand which route he was going to take through the labyrinth of ideas.

2. I cannot be sure, of course, but I think this was yet another thrust at the Swiss.

But distract him – and the effect could be as drastic as with Coleridge when the man from Porlock knocked at the door.[3] He told me the story himself because I used to infuriate him in the beginning. I usually found that if I thought my query intensely enough, he picked it up anyway.

"On the High Ground," he said, as if the words were a proper title. "Some of us are made for the High Ground. We are the ones who must learn to walk with the Gods. On the Middle Ground, there are the ordinary people. The flocks from which the new stock are bred. They breed, they feed, and they heed the words of the Most High."

The Worms
He paused a moment and looked sad. "Then there is the Low Ground. Only one step from the Sea of Oblivion, but people play there who are already blind. Their mothers took them up into the hills, but they ran down again. They are the fodder for the great fishes. They are the ones who gawp at Leviathan in wonder – and forget to run." He shook his head and heaved a huge sigh. "They are the ashes that fall from the alchemical fire. They are the victims."

At the time he said all this, I'll be quite honest about it, I didn't understand. It sounded a bit too much like 'Old Testament Studies' at school. That's why I had a vague idea what Leviathan was. I suppose that is why I remembered it. But Aleister had a way of making his words sink in deeply. It would have been hard not to remember.

I can say that so airily because I remember so much. My head is still full of our conversations. But then, who can ever know how much he may have forgotten? I believe that he still prompts me. I am told, by people who are very intimate with me, that I have a tendency to lapse into a mediumistic trance. I don't want to make too much of this because, as far as I am concerned, I just take forty winks. I have apologised for dropping off after a good meal, and the company has just laughed.

On those occasions, it appears that Aleister speaks through me, or, more rarely, takes over my body and uses it as his own. I

3. William Taylor Coleridge (1772-1834) was writing his famous poem 'Kubla Khan', in the heat of inspiration. After he was interrupted by some businessmen from Porlock, he was never able to finish his work.

ought to add that the same thing occurs vis-á-vis other 'spirits' as well. Someone brings a baby to the house and – zap – grandma comes too! It can be very disconcerting.

But when I say that Aleister prompts me, I mean to say that I get quiet clear messages which arrive in my head. Of course, I quiet understand how 'hearing voices' might well be an hallucination. But I *know* that it is 'only in my head' and the message that follows is far from chaotic or meaningless. As my own man, I would not always write some of the passages that flow from my fingers. Take the 'jokes' as an example: some of them I admit are my own, but others seem 'strange'. I cannot erase them though. Even where I truly consider it spoils the flow or intrudes too much – the joke must stay. Sometimes, when I exert a maximum of will-power, I am allowed to move it. But that is all.

It doesn't happen all the time. I don't think there is any call to change the title page, for example, and say that this book is written 'by Amado Crowley, in collaboration with his father'. I think the text is my own work, but very much in the spirit of Aleister, and as I am writing, I get a great many nudges and just a few direct phrases.

I have a feeling that all of that would have been far better left unsaid. I don't think it helps and it might even throw the cat among the pigeons yet again. Crowley says that those pigeons have strange beaks and rather long necks! In some parts of the world the sport is as popular as bull-fighting in Spain. I think he means he is deliberately baiting some of you, so take care.

But all those years ago, when we were talking man to boy, teacher to student, he was trying to put certain principles across. When he seemed to be dividing men into three categories according to their habitat – The High Ground, The Middle Ground, and The Low Ground – he was using a figure of speech. I don't know whether one can rightly claim 'to be' a psychologist after one has retired, but I *was* a psychologist, and it seems to be quite valid to propose that these means of differentiation do exist at a spiritual level.

Doesn't the Christian religion already speak of 'sheep' and 'goats'? Is it such a radical departure to speak of 'sheep', 'goats', and 'shepherds'?

In actual fact though, I think Aleister's idea would fit in better with a slightly different character trait. One school of thought speaks of 'leaders' and 'followers'; so why don't we add one more, asks my father, and let's call them 'quitters'.

Ghosts in Uniform

Between school and university, I did my National Service. Most people said that they hated it. They thought that it spoiled their chance of a good career. Just to be the odd one out, I actually liked it. Once again, all my friends and comrades found that very weird.

Normally, it was the duty of one member of the Fire Picket to use the Tannoy system to wake the camp up at six-thirty in the morning. I must have been a fool to offer, but I proposed to do it on a regular basis and play records for the first half-hour of the day. To make my idea more interesting, I suggested having a 'request box' in the NAAFI, and I would select a programme from among the records that the lower ranks liked. It went very well for a month or two, then the Group Captain sent for me.

"How does it come about," he asked icily, "that with so many louts on the premises, we are getting Litoff's piano concerto, as played by Madame Moura Lympany?"

"That's because it's the second most popular piece of music on the radio, sir," I replied.

"What is the first?"

"Teresa Brewer singing 'Put Another Nickel In'," I answered.

"Which has not been played once this week."

I pretended to be taken aback. "Are you sure, sir?"

"Quite, it's my wife's favourite."

I gulped and tried to put a brave face on it. "I'll see that it's played especially for her," I suggested.

I had invented the Top Twenty before it ever existed, but it was no good though. I was kicked out for fiddling in five of my own choices for every genuine one that came from the box. Still, I bet that most people of my age remember the tune, if not its name.

I have already spoken of the strange events that happened to me as child. The next unusual event happened when I was posted to an RAF camp near to Beverley. What with sentry-go and Fire Picket, one found oneself on duty every six weeks. One spent the night just walking round the camp, checking up on things. Our orders were quite simple: "Keep an eye out for fires,

176

signs of break-in and couples on the nadge!" This was how the Sergeant put it. If we didn't know at the time, we soon found out what the last directive meant. They were at it everywhere – especially behind the Officers' Mess. We were often slipped a shilling to look for fires elsewhere.

En route, we went through the huge airplane hangers. One of these was largely empty because it was run as a workshop where planes were serviced during the day. It was a booming black void and we all but ran through it. But every single time we did pass that way, I heard voices ... and my comrade didn't. After a few months this murmur of voices suddenly became a clamour of cries and shouts of panic, plus one great drawn-out scream. The corporal of the Guard said the hangar had suffered a direct hit during a bombing raid – one man had been killed and many others had been seriously injured.

On another occasion, this time at midday when most people were at the canteen eating their lunch, someone came into the office where I was working alone.

"You lad!" I looked around and there stood a young RAF officer. He held out a five pound note. "Slip up to the mess and get me a packet of fags, will you? Kensitas if they have them."

"I'm not allowed in the officers' mess" I said. "If I go to the NAAFI they'll wonder where the hell I got a five pound note. I'm only paid twenty-eight bob a week."

"Well, get it on tick then. Tell them it's for Colshaw. Old Tom Colshaw. They know me well enough."

I went to the NAAFI and repeated the message to the girl. "Just a jiff," she said, and buzzed the Duty Sergeant. "It's ten Kensitas," was all she said, and put the telephone down. I assumed that the hitch was caused by my asking for credit.

When the Sergeant arrived, he took his hat off because anyone on NAAFI premises was supposed to be off-duty. Since there was a separate Sergeants' Mess, he shouldn't really have been there himself, but I wasn't going to tell him that. He bought me a coffee and we sat down at a quiet table, well away from the juke box.

I was a bit uneasy. It was not often that a Sergeant sat down with you. Even rarer for one of them to buy you a drink. Beside which, I was running an errand. "I'd better be getting back with the snorts, Sarge, or else I'll be in trouble."

177

"No lad, no trouble. I'll come back with you, just in case."

"He's waiting for his fags, " I said.

"Maybe. Maybe. But Flying Officer Tom Colshaw has been dead for six years. He hanged himself after they dropped bombs on his house and killed his family. His grave is in the local cemetery, if you look."

The very next Sunday morning, I hid a packet of Kensitas in the long grass and tidied up the untended grave.

24

KAUKET

Goddess of primal chaos before the sun and truth emerged

The Secret Order

During the war, I once saw him very deeply moved.

"It's like the end of the world," he said gravely, "except that it's not. In America, they are just waking up to orange juice and waffles, safe from all bombs. The only thing they have to fear is cars with other Americans in them. In Australia, they will all be asleep, nestling up to their sheep and dreaming of rabbits with very long tails." He smiled faintly. It was not his best joke. He was not feeling very funny.

"There is hate abroad," he went on. "Make no mistake about it, there is hate with a trumpet striding the streets and a sack of slogans round her neck."[1]

I might have misheard him or else I took him wrongly. He may have said "strumpet" instead of "trumpet; but it is just as likely that he said "megaphone". It makes more sense if he referred to the whore. The more I think about it, the more probable it seems. In either case, I think you'll get the picture. My father was seething with a deep sense of outrage.

There was a long, long pause and then he said: "We must do something about it!"

At the moment, right there and then, I just assumed he meant that we must make sure that the damage of war was repaired. He meant that London, and everywhere else, must be rebuilt. But no, it wasn't as simple as that. His mind was far away, rummaging in the dark corners of the cosmos. He was thinking of the strange order which the Gods had combed out of the tangled chaos. He pondered the sheer power which can be either fertile

---

1. This reminds me very much of George Fox (1624-1691), the Founder of the Quakers, when he walked through the streets of the city crying "Woe unto the bloody city of Lichfield."

or ruinous - a little bit like the Hindu concept of the Lord Siva.

To put it in the simplest terms possible, the Master Therion was toying with the notion of setting up a new occult Order, with new aims and new methods. He had flirted with the possibility for a very long time in fact. Little by little, he was becoming convinced that it might be his spiritual duty. He explained more fully later. He said that he had received some guidance on the topic, and that word had come "*from beyond*".

I remembered it so clearly because it put me in mind of those days when we worked with Churchill and Mountbatten. The laconic telephone calls from "*you know who*"; the pervasive air of strict secrecy, and the orders to speak only in riddles and never to mention real names. At the time, I had been amused. I was a child, remember, and it had been very much a game for me. But in the later days, as we got closer and closer to our final parting, this kind of thing just made me fret.

He had filled my head with a sense of duty. I knew the fine details of many projects that I had to implement if the call came. Every step of my life was planned, always assuming that the gods appointed me as a Master. I was not being brash about it. To put it simply, I was nervous of not doing it right - of causing some huge blunder.

Many years after, when I talked things over with Gerald Yorke, he was able to confirm a certain amount of what I already knew. He explained that he was stocking everything and anything that had to do with Aleister Crowley. He was building an archive which he would leave to the Warburg Institute on his death. I mentioned that I found this a strange thing to do when he had left my father and taken up the path of Buddhism. "Oh", he replied very gently. "We forgave each other a long, long time ago."

He could not remember any reference to this "New Order" among any of his large folders of documents. But he did have knowledge of a certain rumour that had come his way. "Either it exists," he murmured, "Or it does not. In either case, there was no point in his telling me. He knew perfectly well that I wouldn't be able to join."

He padded across the room and came back, putting Aleister's magic wand in my hands. "Tell me the first word that comes into your head," he ordered.

I studied the small head of the iron wand. "Mexico!" I said.

He took the wand from me with a great smile. "Do not tell me anything else," he murmured. "Then I cannot repeat it."

I felt like someone who has just been before a solicitor and made a solemn, legal statement. Evidently, Gerald Yorke was quite satisfied, and he too had received hints of the secret. Being a Buddhist, and an upright, honest gentleman, he did not wish to 'know', since he would be obliged to reply to other people's questions.

The word I had mentioned, Mexico, seemed to have meant a great deal to him. I think that it was at that very moment that he decided privately to consider me as Aleister Crowley's son and magical heir. "If my old friend had reasons to hide you, then I am not going to go against his wishes."

He smiled and put away all the various documents. When it was time to take our leave his embraced me in his arms and said: "I know nothing at all about any New Order, and I have never heard you utter the word 'Mexico'."[2]

Gerald Yorke did inform certain interested parties of my existence, and some of these did make contact at various times. But true to his word, he did not mention "the other matter" and not one of them seemed to be aware of it.

To cut a long story short, Master Therion did found a new order but everyone connected with it was sworn to secrecy. Yes, I quite agree, it all sounds faintly like 'Indiana Jones and the Last Crusade', or a yarn from a Boys' Adventure Book, but as I explained in my earlier book, this was quite typical of my father's character and quite in keeping with his sense of theatre.

The Set-Up

First of all, he had kept in close contact with people that he had come across in several parts of the world. He must have done this with a certain amount of stealth, or else he used some psychic means. In the war years particularly, one did not just get letters from abroad without an official censor casting his eye over them. Besides which, when he was living in Hastings, they would have been remarked on by other people at the address. Well, no matter how he brought it off, he ordered these people to launch his new order, and to do it by setting up occult cells.

2. I believe that Gerald Yorke made an association with the Order of the Lamp of Invisible Light O.L.I.L.

The men who received this commission had the title "*Wise One*" bestowed on them. There were seven of them in all, and they did not know of each other's existence. For some reason or other, he regarded this as of utmost importance. Perhaps it was a safeguard against any infiltration by the enemy or the secret service. On the other hand, if one group could betray another, they would all have fallen like dominoes. Maybe he was just trying to reduce that risk.

As I show in the diagram, there was one group in the North of France and he made contact via a member of the French Resistance in Chartres. This was quite some distance away, but he had good friends there. He was able to get in touch with the Germans via some friends in Zurich. The one in America had to be dealt with by means of the telephone and it always made me smile that he insisted on reversing the charges! Lastly there was someone in Morocco. This was particularly tricky to set up due to the North African campaign during the war.

Each of these persons would use an owl as his mark, in the same way that a bishop uses a cross. The owl has been a symbol of wisdom since antiquity, long before the building of Athens. But because wisdom is almost always connected with the notion of age, these seven Wise Ones would establish seven 'granny' or 'grandma' groups.

As far as humanly possibly, they would be centred on places that my father selected, but they could vary by ten miles (or sixteen kilometres). That was not the end of the complex twists. Once they were strong and thriving, each of the 'granny' groups must establish seven 'mother' groups, though they could use whatever sites they chose, even long distances away. After that there would be 'daughter' groups and so on. All in all, it was just like a vast family.

I think he chose these innocent terms (granny, mother etc.) for two reasons. First, to ensure that there would always be pathways along which help and information could flow. Second, to avoid, as a matter of policy, all and any likeness to other secret orders who had haughty titles, ranks and degrees.

In fact, he wanted to keep the framework simple and friendly, hence this stress on the family. It works out that each Wise One would be responsible for his original group, seven mother groups and forty-nine daughter groups. This makes fifty-seven groups;

and a grand total of three hundred and ninety-nine groups, each with five to fourteen members. If it has worked out as Crowley intended, no better and no worse, then there would now be something over five thousand members. There are gaps in my diagram of course. I have sweated blood trying to remember the few names that I have been able to reproduce. There must be others. I can only invite them to contact me.

The Watch Light
But fifty years is a hell of a long time to survive without a leader. As in any other sort of society, there must have been many comings and goings. Some branches have faded, some have dropped off, and no one can say how many sprouted. But for reasons that only Aleister would have understood, I now make an estimate that there are three hundred and forty-three 'genuine' occult groups.

I don't mean to sound haughty. By 'genuine', I mean those groups that are founded on AC's secret teaching, who respect his wishes, and who have links with that special order. Now that they have been told, it behoves them to think on these things rather deeply. I may have been born on the wrong side of the blankets but I am Aleister Crowley's son and his magical heir. I am willing to welcome any wanderers home.

It goes without saying that many occult groups may have 'drifted off course' since the captain left ship. Impossible to imagine where the Ark would have ended up if Noah had fallen overboard or decided to go for a swim. My father could do very little to make me age more quickly, and knowing how exposed I was, he kept my existence secret. He had made me, to be sure, and it is possible that he made me precisely to fill this role. But he could not declare me a Master. That was outside his power. As a matter of fact, I wavered for many years and finally accepted the call when I realised that it was my duty. I didn't resist out of any sense of de-merit. Alas, I could think only of what I stood to lose in terms of a normal life and happiness.

Neither my father nor I was at fault in this matter. Until the last rumbles of the war had stopped, the gods expected the waiting people to be patient and to manage on their own. Those people are not to blame either. Not unless they have strayed. Moses had been up the mountain for quite a long time too, I

Figure 3.

The order of the
LAMP OF INVISIBLE LIGHT

Mothers: A. BRADFORD (England)
Daughters: Leeds, Doncaster, Oldham
Grand-daughters   THIRSK, SKIPTON, BOLTON, ECCLES, BUXTON

Mothers: B. WORCESTER (England)
Daughters: Walsall, Cheltenham, Oxford
Grand-daughters   MALVERN, STRATFORD-ON-AVON, LEOMINSTER

Mothers: C. LILLE (France)
Daughters: Gent, Calais, Amiens
Grand-daughters   BOULOGNE, DUNKIRK, ARRAS, CHARLEROI

Mothers: D. RODEZ (France)
Daughters: Nimes, Beziers, Toulouse
Grand-daughters   CAHORS, PERPIGNAN, CAP D'AGDE

Mothers: E. MEKNES (Morocco)
Daughters: Fez, Cueta, Malago, Oujda
Grand-daughters   MOSTAGANEM, TANGER, LARACHE

Mothers: F. BOSTON (U.S.A.)
Daughters: Manchester, Syracuse, Baltimore
Grand-daughters   ALBANY, BANGOR, SHERBROOKE, LONDON

Mothers: G. ULM (Germany)
Daughters: Augsburg, Basel, Mannheim
Grand-daughters   LUDWIGSBURG, HEIDELBURG, ZURICH

remember; but calves of gold are out of the question.

I know how hard it can be, being loyal forever. It is every bit as arduous trying to teach students who refuse to leave the play-pen. There is no wrong where no wrong was willed - and one cannot will without knowing. In case there is a wanderer who wants to come home, a lantern has been lit in the window.

Masters are not shepherds any more than students are sheep. That is a wrong analogy because it smacks of bright brain, dim brute, and dominance. A Master is more like a guide who waits patiently on the lower slopes of the Sacred Mountain. There are numerous paths by which one may climb, but only one is correct for you.

Some avenues are so impressive that pilgrims stop climbing and just stare in wonder, which is just as well since they lead nowhere. Other paths are so difficult, one makes frequent stops to rest and to boast of one's prowess.

"The route should be pleasant," says this person.

The Master asks "Why?"

"The way should be a painful test," says that person.

The Master asks "Why?"

"Why, why, why," sneer the lofty scholars. "Is that all that you've got to say?" They look down on him, this so-called Master who is dressed in rags. "Which path is it then that you would recommend?"

"The one that goes to the top," he replies.

They blink in pity and vacancy.[3]

Silent Starlings

As you might expect, I have forgotten so many things that we did together, my father and I. Yet at the same time, I have a very clear memory of others. So many of his sayings have slipped my mind, while others are branded there. Have I been careless? I tend to wonder. Why did I cherish one memory and neglect so many others? I suppose that there was some difference and that it mattered to a child of that age.

The vital things seems to be - how I reacted at the time, and that has nothing to do with how old I am now. What was it that managed to catch my imagination - the one sweet that was

---

3. In the shrine at the top of Mount Fujiyama, in Japan, the following words are inscribed. "Men climb by many routes to look at the same moon."

wrapped in red paper - a sledge called 'Rosebud'? When I was young, some things were already important and I had given them a special niche in my mind.

This was exactly the case with my father. The things I remember most clearly are those that are linked with something else which may or may not have been relevant but which struck me as vivid. It could be a place, a face, a noise or a reverie but my mind grabbed it and used it to mark the calendar. As I worked on the first book, I was boggled by the sheer quantity of material that came flooding back. Much of it was a motley mixture of images without any sort of pattern to them. It was like emptying a rag-bag onto the floor. The bits to do with cloaks and daggers drew my eye first.

But then, as I sorted through them, the less obvious ones took on more and more meaning. Once I overcame my own doubts, I found that one door opened on to others. I don't recall the exact date. He was still living at Jermyn Street, in central London. During the night there had been a very bad air-raid. The bombs had dropped without let-up but we slept quite soundly in a shelter in the cellars. Next morning, we listened to the news on the radio, and he decided to take me to the East End. He wanted me to see the damage that had been done.

I was quite nervous. I couldn't help but think that they might come back even in daylight. I was nervous that any strange object might be a time bomb or deadlier still, a booby trap. There had been a lot of posters warning about the latest menace - a thing that we called a 'butterfly'. On hitting the ground it was meant to open up and display a curious shape that was very alluring to children. No, I was far from happy about this visit.

You might have expected the police to be in charge, keeping the streets free and aiding the fire engines to get through. But it was total chaos and it was spread over such a wide area that everyone was engaged on rescuing those who were still alive. Several houses had been knocked flat, but most of them looked half unfixed, as if a willful child had kicked his meccano set.

I remember a lavatory jutting out from one wall, and the roll of toilet paper was still burning. But most of all I remember the people, some of whom were just walking in circles, like Saturday night drunks who had forgotten where they lived. There was weeping, very quiet weeping, and then, suddenly, there'd be some shouting followed by a deathly hush. Just the wind, the crackle of charring wood, as men faltered out of the ruins with a draped stretcher.

We didn't go to gawp at the wreckage. We weren't looking for the kind of thrill[4] you get at seeing harm done to others when you have escaped. We went in homage, I think.

"I want you to look," he said, "and I want you to remember. This was done by demi-gods who ordered the sun to stop."

The oddest thing was that there were birds about, thousands of them, but they no longer sang. Telephone wires that still stood were thick with starlings but they were silent. It was as if nature herself were confused and did not know what to do. My father bent down and picked up a celluloid[5] doll. He held it in both hands and gazed at its poor, squashed face.

"This sorry object has been very much loved," he mumbled as he pressed it tightly to his chest. "One knows not where she is. But she would love to have this with her."

He laid it on a big stone. It burst into flame and left no mark.

"They used to sicken me," he mourned, "those words they carve on certain tombs, like Together Again." He lifted his head and his eyes swept bleakly over the scene of bad deeds and iniquity.

"But now, we must put it all together again."

We both wept.

4. The Germans have a name for it: schadenfreude.
5. One of the earliest forms of plastic, made from camphor and cellulose nitrate. Highly inflammable.